Thinking about Music

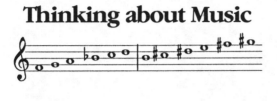

Ross Lee Finney, Ann Arbor, studio, mid-1960s. At work.

33.50

DUE DATE

FEB 2 2 1996		
201-6503		Printed in USA

Thinking

about

Music

The Collected Writings of Ross Lee Finney

Edited and with a Preface by Frederic Goossen

The University of Alabama Press • Tuscaloosa and London

The paper on which this book is printed meets the minimum requirements of American National Standard for Information Science-Permanence of Paper for Printed Library Materials, ANSI A39.48-1984.

Library of Congress Cataloging-in-Publication Data

Finney, Ross Lee, 1906–
    [Literary works.   Selections]
    Thinking about Music: The Collected Writings of Ross Lee Finney / edited, and with a preface, by Frederic Goossen.
        p.   cm.
    Includes bibliographical references (p.   ).
    ISBN 0-8173-0521-1 (permanent paper)
    1. Music—History and criticism.   I. Goossen, Frederic.
    II. Title.
    ML60.F54   1991   90-11104
    780—dc20   CIP
                                                                       MN

British Library Cataloguing-in-Publication Data available

To Shirley.

Contents

Preface ix

Acknowledgments xv

Part I: **On Learning and Teaching**

1. The Composer and the University 3
2. The Uniqueness of Musical Craft 12
3. The Value of the Abstract 31
4. Education and the Creative Imagination in Music 47
5. Employ the Composer 56
6. The Artist Must Rebel 62
7. Making Music 70

Part II: **On Music and Culture**

8. Modern Chamber Music in American Culture 83
9. The Relation of the Performer to the American Composer 91
10. The Composer and Society: The Composer's Unique Relation to His Culture 96
11. Music and the Human Need 103
12. America Goes West 119

Part III: **On Composing**

13. The Composer Speaks: The Piano Quintet 127
14. Analysis and the Creative Process 130
15. Problems and Issues Facing American Music Today 147
16. The Diversity of Inculturation 152
17. Composing Music for Dance 158
18. A Composer's Perception of Time 163
19. Musical Complementarity 169

Part IV: **Coda**

20. Landscapes Remembered: Memory and Musical
    Continuity 177
Notes 187
Appendix A 199
Appendix B 202

Preface

Most composers believe that their works should speak for them. Few are notably voluble either about themselves or other topics, although when they do speak, often they have interesting and original things to say. In our century such masters as Igor Stravinsky in the *Poetics of Music*; Roger Sessions in *The Musical Experience of Composer, Performer, Listener*; Paul Hindemith in *A Composer's World: Horizons and Limitations*; and Aaron Copland in *Music and Imagination* have demonstrated uncommon skill in verbal expression while enriching our understanding of the creative mind and its ways.

The association of composers, especially in the United States, with institutions of higher education has encouraged them to speak and write more consistently than in the past. The life of a professor necessarily involves talking and writing, and this remains true even if one pursues the career of composer simultaneously. Thus American composers as a group are somewhat more eloquent than their predecessors. A tongue-tied composer in our day finds himself at a disadvantage.

Fortunately, circumstances and natural inclination combined to lend Ross Lee Finney the capacity to express himself clearly and directly, and the opportunity to do so. As a result, there exists a considerable body of material from which to select a representative group of essays, lectures, speeches, and other writings to support and enhance his stature as composer and teacher. The gathering of this material into a book offers those who are interested in American music, in modern music, and in the development of American musical education the perspective of one of the seminal figures in the musical life of this country in the twentieth century. In many ways, Ross Lee Finney is the quintessential American composer. His dual career as composer and developer of young composers exemplifies the ideal of the composer in the university, although Finney never was an "academic composer." He maintained a balance between creative and academic life, succeeding in a difficult enterprise that has thwarted many an American composer.

Born in Wells, Minnesota, December 23, 1906, reared in Valley City, North Dakota, and Minneapolis, where he studied under Donald N. Ferguson at the University of Minnesota, Finney received his bachelor of arts degree from Carleton College. After study with Nadia Boulanger and Alban Berg in Europe, Finney returned home to a career as composer and professor that has spanned six decades. He remains active as composer, visiting artist, member of musical and cultural organizations and boards, observer and commentator upon American music and culture. He is a continuing force in contemporary life. His vision, insight, and occasional bluntness are bracing elements in the musical world. There is no one quite like him on the American scene.

When the School of Music of The University of Alabama inaugurated its Endowed Chair in Music in the academic year 1982–83 with the intent to appoint a composer to that position, Finney's name surfaced at once. We sought an eminent American composer whose experience included success as a teacher, and no one fit that description quite so well as Finney, whose twenty-six years at the University of Michigan had placed him among the most distinguished mentors of young composers in American musical history. He seemed the logical choice to lend distinction and substance to our Chair.

During his year at Alabama, all who came into contact with Finney were warmed at the fire of his enthusiasm, as they were inspired by his dedication to music and musical composition. Not only the young composers who studied under him, but the whole musical and academic community felt the exhilarating effect of his presence.

This volume of Finney's writings, spanning nearly fifty years, is one of the products of his year at Alabama. From among his many essays, public lectures and speeches, twenty titles have been selected to express the essence of Finney's thoughts about music and culture, some appearing here for the first time in print. Although the writings constitute a collection, there is a clear progression from an early emphasis upon distinctive Americanism in music, through the exploration of serialism in the 1950s, to the experimental radicalism of the 1960s. In the most recent decade there appear a notable serenity and a high degree of integration. Because the book is a collection, occasionally some redundancies surface, for Finney naturally returns to ideas that hold special significance for him. A particular example is his concern with what he calls "musical complementarity," the method of composing with symmetrical hexachords which he discusses in different ways in "Making Music," "Musical Complementarity," and "Landscapes Remembered."

The titles are arranged in three main groups, chosen to exhibit the extent of Finney's professional life and interests. Within a group, titles are ordered chronologically, each date noted at the end. This organization enables readers interested in principal topics to find their way, while following the development of Finney's thinking. Those who prefer a chronology of the whole are referred to Appendix A, where the dates of all titles are given. The collection ends with a "coda," the lecture "Landscapes Remembered: Memory and Musical Continuity," delivered without notes at Alabama and transcribed from tape recording by the editor. Such materials as I deemed essential to understanding or elucidating Finney's meaning, along with the sources of his references to writers of many eras, are collected in the Notes.

Part I: On Learning and Teaching, presents Finney's ideas about musical education in the American university. He accepts the concept of music as an integral part of education, recognizing the difference between American policy and the separation of music as a profession from music as a scholarly pursuit characteristically European. He argues in favor of placing the composer, and creative imagination, at the center of musical education. Such an idea flies in the face of American practice, where music as performance and recreation plays a dominant role, but it suggests why Finney was a "pied piper" to generations of young composers during his tenure at Michigan. He is a natural leader.

Finney's teaching must have been compelling, if "The Uniqueness of Musical Craft" can serve as an example. In discussing Hindemith's *Mathis der Maler* Symphony, he explains how a composer might translate extra-musical suggestion into musical terms, basing his exposition on Hindemith's tonal theories. His analysis is technical, never deviating from the musical text.

Throughout Part I, Finney emphasizes that music is essential to a humanistic education, its creative element is fundamental to such an education, the university is responsible to nurture the creative imaginations of its students, such nurture should begin in infancy, and the study of music as a serious art and discipline need not be confined to those who intend to pursue it professionally. His intent always is to understand music as one of the great symbolic languages of humankind and to present it in that light.

In Part II: On Music and Culture, Finney appears as commentator on a wider range of subjects. He is unselfconsciously American, unsentimental in his understanding of the difficulties American society has experienced in coming to terms with the fine arts, impatient with the ivory-towerism that so often has impeded the development of serious music in this country, insistent that music be valued for its intrinsic worth, and perceptive in his recognition of the potential of composers whose later work was to validate his judgment.

Finney demonstrates his belief that the education of a composer should not be confined to professional training by the wide range of references to writers as different as Descartes and Lewis Mumford. Part II closes with "America Goes West," in the course of which Finney refers approvingly to composers as diverse as Roger Sessions, Virgil Thomson, Aaron Copland, John Cage, Milton Babbitt, Andrew Imbrie, Leon Kirchner, Morton Feldman, Earle Brown, and Roger Reynolds. Not many commentators in 1967 would have been able to see merit in the work of everyone on that list.

Because Ross Lee Finney has kept his original dedication to composition at the center of his life, Part III: On Composing, is the culmination of this book. It is a series of musings on the elusive subject of what composing is and how one does it. Composers, never the most articulate of artists, are especially reticent when discussing how they work. Finney himself notes this tendency in the first sentence of "The Composer Speaks."

Nevertheless, he here offers insight into the germination, development, and realization of musical compositions. He makes no claim that his way is the only way, although his confidence in his methods and their outcome is apparent everywhere, and the rich musical results do, indeed, speak for themselves.

Part III of the book covers some thirty-five years of the composer's life. Of particular interest are "Analysis and the Creative Process," and "Musical Complementarity." Each is devoted to painstaking discussion of some of the most intimate and intriguing aspects of the process of composing. In the first of these Finney describes the genesis of two different works, both derived from the same source. His conviction that composing is the indivisible combination of reason and emotion serves as the basis for explaining the process that produced his String Quintet and Second Symphony.

In "Musical Complementarity," Finney discusses his method, developed over nearly forty years, of reconciling total chromaticism with tonality. He traces his belief in the compatibility of chromaticism with a sense of tonal center, or "pitch polarity," back to his studies with Alban Berg in the 1930s. Berg was the only one of Arnold Schoenberg's early associates who refused to abandon tonality despite adopting chromatic serialism. His teaching, in Finney's memory, connected serialism firmly with tonality.

Finney states that his own music is not serial, but that it is tonal. It is based on his system of symmetrical hexachords, which governs the microcosmic order. The larger structural order is founded on tonality, a system of principal pitches that provides the "polar" points of the design. This "complementarity" between the two levels of musical order lends tension and articulation to the form. It is notable that none of Part III requires sophisticated technical knowledge for comprehension. Finney explains complex musical concepts so that the interested nonprofessional can grasp them.

The book closes with "Landscapes Remembered: Memory and Musical Continuity." In transcribing this lecture I have kept as much of the spontaneity of the moment as was appropriate to a printed text. Finney likes to lecture without notes, and what may sometimes be lost in conventional exposition is more than compensated for by the mercurial weavings of an original and fascinating mind. One of Finney's chief interests in the past few years has centered upon memory and the ways in which it can be exploited to achieve coherence in musical compositions. This lecture deals with that question by way of his work for small orchestra, *Landscapes Remembered*, among his most poignant and beautiful scores. It seemed a fitting envoi to the book.

No artist, and no artist's work, can be summed up in a simple statement. Still, every artist of consequence projects a definite profile. The elements of Finney's personality that dominate are intelligence, lucidity, ebullience, optimism, and determination. He has worked for the better part of a century to produce music of a high order, a body of work that looms large on the American musical horizon with growing influence and prestige a certainty. Some of the sources of that music are revealed and discussed in the pages of this book. The essential characteristics of its creator's mind and sensibility are displayed here clearly and uncompromisingly.

These essays and lectures, in their concern for musical learning and teaching, for music rooted in our culture yet making no compromises, and for the development of individual style based on complete mastery of craft together with reliance upon intuition, are the work and thought of an artist whose contribution to American music is exemplary. In his life and in his work, Ross Lee Finney is an American original.

Frederic Goossen
Tuscaloosa, Alabama

Acknowledgments

Among the pleasures of preparing a manuscript for publication is the recognition of those who have provided help along the way. Research on this book proved to be more demanding and frequently more elusive than I had expected. Without the aid of the friends and colleagues noted here, the book would not have reached completion.

I wish to thank in particular Ross Lee and Gretchen Ludke Finney for their patient and cheerful advice and assistance at every stage of the project, and for the use of photographs from their private collection. They went far out of their way to help.

Especially helpful in locating obscure pieces of information for the Notes were Charles Sems, Music Specialist, Library of Congress; Howard Boatwright, Professor Emeritus, Syracuse University; Rosemary Cullen, Curator of the Harris Collection in the John Hay Library, Brown University; and Barbara Filipac, Senior Library Associate Specialist in Manuscripts, also of the John Hay Library at Brown; Corey Field, Director of Publications and Marketing, European-American Music Distributors Corporation; Leslie C. McCall, Reference/Music Librarian, Amelia Gayle Gorgas Library, The University of Alabama; Angela Jenkins Wright, Supervisor/Librarian, Interlibrary Loan Office, University Libraries, The

University of Alabama; and Christel A. Bell, The University of Alabama.

Also to be noted for aid in verifying circumstances surrounding the original presentation of many parts of the book are Ann Flowers, Assistant Archivist, Michigan Historical Collection, Bentley Library, University of Michigan; Sandra Garstang, Library Assistant, Robert Millikan Library, California Institute of Technology; William McClellan, Music Librarian, School of Music, University of Illinois; Judy Harvey Sahak, Librarian of the Denison Library, Scripps College; and Jerry Thornton, Technical Library Assistant, Harlan Hatcher Graduate Library, University of Michigan. To my editor, Eunice H. Payne, I owe special thanks for her sharp eyes and skilled professional advice. And I thank Gary R. Smoke, who prepared the musical examples.

Finally, I offer my thanks to my wife, Shirley Reed Goossen, whose indefatigable aid and good humor kept the project firmly on track. Her research for the Notes, her preparation of the typescript, and above all her many intelligent and thoughtful suggestions combined to improve the book immeasurably.

Whatever faults remain are my responsibility.

Part I

On Learning and Teaching

1

The Composer and the University

It is the common belief of musicians that their art should hold a larger place in the humanities than it does. The high position that music held in the medieval university is misleading, but it is true that music, as an art, has lost status in modern society. Music as an accomplishment and a recreation is greatly valued, and we feel no real antagonism from our colleagues in the humanities as long as we remain within those limits. But such a position frustrates scholarship, belittles performance, and mocks the importance of a creative environment in the university. It is only natural, therefore, that scholar, performer, and composer should seek in common to raise the esteem in which their art is held.

This common purpose should unify those musicians who find themselves sheltered by the academic environment, but in fact it does not. The musicologist asserts that only through the discipline of scholarship can a level of musical integrity be achieved which will meet the requirements for learning in a great university. This position follows Matthew Arnold's dictum that "all learning is scientific which is systematically laid out and followed up to its original sources, and that a genuine humanism is scientific."[1]

The performer (and I am referring to the thinking performer) leans toward the position that one learns by doing, and that only through the act of music-making does one gain knowledge of the art. Thus, performance is to music what laboratory experiment is to science and should occupy the same position in the curriculum. I fear that this attitude would not be shared by Thomas Huxley, but the performer might gain solace from that gentleman's insistence upon the practical.

Now, in all this rivalry the composer's position has not been well defined. Our dignity has not been questioned. We seem always to be accepted into the assemblies of the learned in this country. We are told now and then that we are really musicologists, though we know better. Periodically we move over into the ranks of the performers, but not too successfully, I believe. The theorist fears but tolerates us. We are a floating population in the American university, traditionally the oldest segment of that community, and respected in a dignified way, but not understood and, I think, not appreciated.

For it is in the creative process that art makes its unique contribution to the university. All learning may be scientific that is systematically laid out and followed up to its original sources, as Arnold says, but in systematizing learning the individual must understand what he hears and sees in terms of his own experience. He must be aware of his own frame of reference for his observations to be relevant. This awareness of self is an essential part of the creative process.

Dr. George F. F. Lombard of Harvard University develops an argument in his article "Self-Awareness and Scientific Method" that even in the physical sciences a factor enters into the controlled experiment that reflects the investigator's capacity to relate facts to his general experience.[2] The scientist may call this process a "hunch," and belittle it as though he wished not to admit that intuitive judgment had affected his results. Scientific writing frequently resorts to such phrases as "at some time and in some way not recorded," or "a small thing; random; inexplicable.[3] Now, when we can control the variables. . . ."[4] It becomes apparent that without a frame of reference, without knowledge of the way in which the individual affects his material, data even in the natural sciences is suspect. In the social sciences, writes Lombard, this "balance in the processes of the mind that leads to effective awareness"[5] is essential to any research.

> Consequently, balanced awareness involves an effective alternation between reflective thinking and concentrated attention. . . . The difficulty of acquiring an awareness of one's own frames of reference is great. . . . It is nonetheless inevitable in the accumulation of knowledge; else the researcher fails to separate what he brings to the situation from the data he is studying.
> . . . Awareness of self increases our capacity for handling ourselves in relation to our data by forcing on us continuous and critical inner appraisal and reappraisal of what we are doing in relation to an external reality.[6]

Clearly, the development of an awareness of self is of the greatest importance and value to a student.

The relating of "self" to material is the common practice of the creative artist. Only as the artist can give new significance to the traditional material that he inherits can he hope to assume an important creative position. He must constantly accept or refuse to accept material that comes to his mind, and the resulting balance that he achieves is his own personal "style." This personal style is no more than the reflection in his art of his self-awareness; no more than the result of a selection made on the basis of his frame of reference. However difficult may be the acquisition of an awareness of one's own frame of reference, the artist must acquire it, for it is the essential part of individuality and self-expression.

We sometimes talk about the intuitive processes of the artist as being so far removed from the "controlled experiments" of the scientist as to exclude the composer, the painter, and the writer from the learned community. But is the artist's process of mind so far removed from that of the scientist? Is not the difference largely one of data studied, and of the artist's even greater need for the use of intuitive judgment?

I am not interested in claiming that the artist is a scientist. Obviously he is not. He is almost the exact opposite. What I do claim is that the intuitive judgment of the artist is an exceedingly and increasingly important process of thought even in science, and that often, particularly in the fields of language and social relationships, it might be almost as important to understand how the composer arrives at his choice of material as to learn through laboratory technique the methods of controlled experiment.

The fundamental task of teaching music in the university is to introduce the student to a language of emotional expression. Any language is a living thing, and of all the phenomena of human behavior, perhaps the most difficult to study by the process of controlled experiment alone. We all know that if we are to investigate the subtle complexities of musical language we must relate it to the living art of music that the student musician knows. We must achieve the "self-awareness" of which Lombard speaks.

Arnold says the same thing when he speaks of "relating what we have learnt and known to the sense which we have in us for conduct, to the sense which we have in us for beauty."[7] The scientist talks about frames of reference and the poet about the sense of beauty, but they are both talking about essentially the same thing.

Lombard criticizes the social scientist for his failure to understand the limitations of the controlled experiment as a method of studying human behavior, and he particularly condemns the tendency of the investigator to escape the problem by studying data far removed from the realities of modern life. As Lombard says,

> We study situations far removed from what is familiar to us because we hope that the gross determinants of the behavior occurring in them will persist and be obvious to the investigator in spite of his presence. [Or] We retreat into a pseudo-objectivity that defeats itself. By attempting to make our . . . experiments completely objective, we arrive at a typical norm so far removed from the uniqueness of the particular instance that the knowledge gained is all but useless in application.[8]

I cannot escape the impression that exactly the same thing happens in the study of musical language. Either we study an ancient style without correlating the materials with a modern frame of reference, or we seek an objective approach to the musical language that sterilizes the material for modern expression. The teacher of theory has drifted too often into the position of seeming to be unaware of the need for the student to relate the material to his own personal experience as a musician. Both in sociology and in music the cause is the same: an exaggeration of the importance of the scientific method.

The fallacy of our day is the scientific approach to all learning. The fallacy comes not from the method, but from the manner in which the method is applied. The tone of our universities has changed fundamentally in the past century because of the concept of the scientific approach. The humanities have not always kept to their broad field of human thought but have deserted to the narrower ways of the scientific approach, hoping to find there the comforts of a discipline as exact as that of the natural sciences. But what is needed today is not science but humanism, and the great danger is that the humanities may have lost their capacity to give us what we need.

We are coming to understand that the scientific method alone cannot solve the problems that we face. As Merle A. Tuve, the distinguished American physicist, states:

> The current great public emphasis on research and science with vast sums being poured into development laboratories for purposes which the public understands in terms of technological goals . . . is a risky and unbalanced situation. . . . The real unbalance lies in the overwhelming emphasis which is given to practical matters and material things in contrast to things of the spirit. The really outstanding need of today lies squarely in the field of humanities.[9]

I would add to his statement: a humanities not sterilized by scientific method, but humanized by the development of an awareness of modern needs.

The unique contribution of the creative artist is his dedication to a living, modern humanism. I would point out that only one dictionary definition of the word "humanism" involves the ancient classics; another, and the one I refer to, is "that attitude of thought or action centering upon distinctively human interests or ideals, esp. as contrasted with naturalistic or religious interests."[10] The composer, guardian of the art of music as a living expression of human feeling, must be an essential part of the university if humanism is to be a living discipline.

Let me turn from the general to the specific. There are many ways in which the composer affects the university community, but I am concerned particularly with his relation to the teaching of language—to the teaching of the theory of music. It is my contention that scientific method has had a very damaging effect upon the teaching of musical theory and that the composer must speak out against it. For the sake of perspective, it might be valuable to consider for a moment the effect of scientific method on another language—for example, on the field of English.

The university English department is concerned with teaching both the critical study of literature and the practical writing of the language. Critical and historical study in literature is based on a scholarly method that has been broadly influenced by scientific research techniques. Writing the language, however, has remained an art. The English department recognizes the fact that the craft of writing is not scientific, and that the grounds for judgment are often intuitive. To be sure, there are rules of grammar such as the one that every sentence should contain a verb, but this rule is not usually considered a law of nature. It is a tradition, and when a James Joyce breaks that tradition the teaching profession adjusts itself as best it can.

I know of no scholar who has organized the relation of conjunctions to adverbs into classifications on the basis, let us say, of selected scenes from Shakespeare, and then on the basis of that tabulation, which would possess little enough validity as a scientific method, has postulated a procedure for the teaching of writing to college freshmen. The English department has wisely kept the scientific method out of classes on writing the language. The teacher has sought instead those verities that we inherit from the past to help expression, to clarify logic, to promote consistency and economy of style.

Within the past century the scholarly method of dealing with music literature has made great strides, and the musicologist has taught us how to undertake a critical study of musical style. But unlike the scholar of English literature, he has not always realized the limitations of his discipline as a method of teaching the craft of musical language. The danger is perhaps not so great when the teacher is a scholar of unquestioned integrity, but when his scholarship is based upon a pseudoscientific approach, his influence on the teaching of theory can be truly pernicious.

Once the musicologist has examined an ancient musical style, as the sociologist might a primitive society, he is tempted to carry his study over into the field of pedagogy, for we all know that the writing of textbooks is a lucrative occupation. Let me point out a typical example, and one on such a high level of scholarship that criticism seems almost insulting.

The Danish musicologist Knud Jeppesen published an admirable and definitive study of the style of Palestrina.[11] This volume is a landmark in the field of musicological research, and invaluable both as an approach to the music of Palestrina and as an example of method to be used in the study of other styles. Jeppesen followed this analytical study with a textbook on counterpoint based on Palestrina's style, a text which is today, either in its original form or in lesser adaptations, commonly used in our music schools.[12]

As I have pointed out, no English department ever would think of teaching the technique of writing on the basis of a critical study of Shakespeare's style. Jeppesen, unfortunately, succumbed to the textbook temptation, and students still are trying to adapt his method to their own frames of reference. They will not suffer too greatly from this study if they will go back to Jeppesen's earlier volume to find in Palestrina's music those verities of good melody that apply to a modern composer as much as to an ancient one. They may find something that will help them to become more aware of musical language. The value will come not from trying to write as Palestrina did, however interesting that might be, but from the development of a viewpoint that frees the student from chordal thinking. Jeppesen's *Counterpoint* may represent a direction that is regrettable in modern musical pedagogy, but there is nothing false in his scholarship.

The same cannot be said for other volumes that are widely

used to teach musical theory. One in particular comes to mind that attempts on the basis of a stylistic analysis of the Bach chorales to project not only a method for the scholarly evaluation of all styles of eighteenth-century music, but also a procedure for the mastery of the basic harmonic language of today.[13] It is like the famous elixir that guarantees to cure frostbite and throws in for good measure all gastrointestinal maladies.

This volume undertakes far more than does Jeppesen, and on a much narrower scholarly basis, for the author had not previously written a definitive stylistic study of Bach's music. If we are to find the scholarly basis for this work, we must seek it in the textbook itself. While we find all the trappings of the scientific method, we seek in vain for any profound study. The mania for tabulation, so typical of the scientific fixation, is found here on almost every page, but the philosophy of the book is as academic and sterile as that of Percy Goetschius.[14] The book might well be entitled *Classification of Chords in 371 Bach Chorales*. Like Jeppesen's *Counterpoint*, it confounds scientific method with art.

Textbooks such as these, based on enthusiasm for pseudoscientific method and used so liberally in our music schools, hinder students from relating the language of music to their own experience. Such books are retrogressive, since they defeat the student in his search for a self-awareness that can alert him to the expressive power of music.

I have mentioned this matter of textbooks in the field of musical theory because it seems to me a notable area in which the impact of scientific method has done injury to the art. While the number of students engaged in learning to speak and to understand the language of music always will be much smaller than that studying the languages of daily communication, nevertheless the problems of teaching will remain the same, and it is time that composers spoke out against a method of pedagogy in musical theory based on pseudoscientific procedure. The English department has cast off the stiff methods of rhetoric, but even those were more realistic than some that are being used to teach music. As I have said, I know of no English teacher who would for a moment accept the codification of an ancient style as the basis for teaching the living language.

The composer is the guardian of creative thought in music. It is he who asserts the importance of art as a living part of civilization. He is not concerned with the moving of bones from one graveyard to another. He *is* concerned with the expression of emotion, and with the craft that communicates that expression to others. He is concerned with values. While he criticizes the clichés that make art banal, at the same time he preserves the traditions of art that are potent.

The creative artist does not compete with the scholar. The scholar's field is the critical interpretation of the past, and a scholar can be as creative as a composer. The composer is concerned with an entirely different aspect of the human mind—its capacity to evolve new expression. A university dedicated only to the investigation of the past is indeed an institution of dead learning, and no American university intentionally dedicates itself to such a purpose. It is important, therefore, that the creative artist function actively in our intellectual communities. It is far less dangerous to the integrity and purpose of the university to award a few prizes for creative thought than, out of fear, to close the academic doors to living art.

Jacques Barzun ends his book *Teacher in America* with this statement: "I would urge the artists to become aggressive, to make converts. They will be the first to benefit, and we may then see that miracle hoped for but never realized, of the university sheltering living genius—not merely canonizing the dead."[15]

There is too much talk of the university as the patron of the arts. The creative artist in America does not ask for patronage. He seeks to contribute to that spiritual element of our culture without which we are doomed. He seeks to help correct the imbalance which materialism has inflicted upon us. He seeks to assume the position which is his by right in the education of the young, to foster that enthusiasm for inspirational values that flows from art. He seeks to assert everlastingly that the humanities are alive, that the humanities are a vibrant heritage, one that can affect our lives as profoundly as science.

(1950)

2

The Uniqueness of Musical Craft

In an attempt to understand the community of the arts, scholars often seek parallels hoping to find that the methods of expression in one art will illuminate methods in another. We cannot deny that the creative artist, whatever his medium, attempts, through symbols of one sort or another—through language—to give statement to the ideas and feelings that all of us have, to a degree, in common. To quote Lewis Mumford: "If man has surpassed his animal destiny, it is because he has utilized the dream and the word to open up territory that cannot be reached on foot or opened up with ax or plow. He has learned to ask questions for which, in the limits of a single lifetime or a single epoch of culture [and I might add, the medium of a single art] he will never find the answer."[1] And so it would be as senseless to think of the arts as unrelated as it would be senseless to think them separate from human emotions. The job of the scholar may very well be to relate the arts and to study them as part of the history of ideas.

The creative artist, on the other hand, concerned as he is with the minute problems of his own language, usually will seek to emphasize that which is unique to his own craft. The composer's general remarks on aesthetics are likely to be less illuminating than his comments on the specific problems of writing music. It is asking too much to expect of the composer that catholicity of taste and balanced judgment so essential for the scholar, and perhaps it is essential even to the scholar's work to emphasize the unique qualities of music and the specific qualities of individual style.

In discussing what is unique in musical craft, one necessarily is concerned with that part of music that is consciously fabricated. Not that one can draw the line very clearly between inspiration and the "application of the seat of the pants to the seat of the chair,"[2] but one is best able to analyze the workings of the creative mind at those moments when the mind is most at work. For this reason one should not dwell on certain elements of music that are very important, such as melody and rhythm. Melody, like line in painting, can be a sudden flash of inspiration or the result of infinite study and care. Rhythm too has many qualities not all of which are developed intuitively by the artist. But both melody and rhythm, important as they are to music, offer less striking contrasts to the other arts than do the devices of tonal orientation that the composer commands. Uniqueness in musical craft can best be studied in that area where intuitive judgment is less likely to play a role than it does in melody and rhythm.

No aspect of the composer's technique is so conscious as the focusing of general pitch—the establishment of tonal level. Herein lies the aspect of craft that is most peculiar to music. I do not say that it has no parallel in the other arts. The spatial concept of form that concerned Cézanne probably is closely akin to tonal organization, and perhaps plot, as so cogently described by E. M. Forster in *Aspects of the Novel*, is very similar, but I need only mention painting and literature for the differences to be apparent.[3] Tonality has two aspects: time and pitch level, and thereby enters the psychological problem of association or memory that crystallizes the two into a monumental—perhaps I should say *imagined* monumental—entity. This is the quality of musical craft that is unlike the other arts, and in the devices of tonality we may find that which is unique to music.

Theorists have dealt too little with the development of the concept of tonality. There is still a great deal to be learned from analytical study of the music of the seventeenth century, that period of shift from modality to tonality. Particularly as a background to the major conflict of our time between the concepts of tonality and atonality would such research be valuable. We need to know what has been and is now meant by tonality before we use such labels as atonality, extended tonality, and polytonality. The meaning of tonality is still likely to be understood as synonymous with key or root as it was defined in nineteenth-century harmony books, but surely such a limited definition is not acceptable. Could it not be argued that Schoenberg's twelve-tone technique is not so much concerned with tonality as with the integration of chromaticism and counterpoint, with a suggestion of new associative devices—new methods of melodic variation—to take the place of fugue and canon? Schoenberg would not agree. He wrote unequivocally that "during a period of approximately twelve years, I laid the foundations for a new procedure in musical construction which seemed fitted to replace those structural differentiations provided formerly by tonal harmonies."[4] He developed a system that was intended to replace the conscious device of tonal organization.

I have mentioned Schoenberg merely to point out how essential is an understanding of the unique craft of tonality if we are to understand the problems of music in our time. No one can understand the implications of the twelve-tone technique without a real understanding of the manner in which a composer uses tonal focus to heighten the meaning of musical function. Such understanding may lead one to see in the devices of technique not a limitation of tonality, but an expansion of that traditional craft.

It is my purpose to try to clarify this fundamental technique of the composer. I wish to approach the problem in such a way as to point out that this aspect of craft is unique to music. It would be ideal to select a musical composition inspired by another art and to see how the composer has translated the symbols of another art, consciously or unconsciously, into musical devices.

We know perfectly well that most music is not inspired by other arts but springs directly from a desire to express in its own terms. We run the risk, in making a comparison of one art with another, of establishing a false dichotomy. It is important to remember that the formal organization of music is largely abstract. If we keep this fact in mind, we can gain a clearer understanding of how the composer has worked and can see the outside force that influenced his choice of material.

There are many works that we could choose, but few so ideally suited to our purpose as Paul Hindemith's symphony *Matthias the Painter.* Here is a work in which the inspiration is definite, available for us to examine, and visual rather than audible. It is common knowledge that the great *Isenheim Altar* painted by Matthias Grünewald served as Hindemith's point of departure. There are undoubtedly many works both contemporary and classic that we could choose but few where the association can be followed so clearly.

I shall point out first the formal organization and the contrasts of mood that the painter Grünewald used in his great work and then suggest the devices that Hindemith used to translate these values into musical ones. I shall even suggest a symbolism in Hindemith's score that is very rare in music, and that I shall base not only on an analysis of the relation of the musical structure of the symphony to the meaning of the paintings but also on Hindemith's own comments concerning another of his works. I do not wish to put too much emphasis on symbolism. My intention is to clarify what the composer means when he speaks of tonal architecture. I wish to show that this organization in music is more than the orientation of chords, and that dissonance, at least in Hindemith's mind, does not, as Schoenberg says, "renounce a tonal center."[5]

Perhaps I should mention some facts concerning this symphony's origin. It was made from incidental music taken from Hindemith's own opera *Matthias the Painter*, which he composed in 1933 but which was not performed until 1938 in Zürich after the composer had been forced to leave Germany. The libretto for this opera is based upon some of the facts that are known about the great German painter, Matthias Grünewald, or more properly Matthias Gothart Nithart, who was born probably in Würzburg about 1465. This painter, who was for so long forgotten and sometimes even confused with Dürer, has come to be appreciated during our century as one of the most forceful artists of his day. Very little is known about his life, but from the little that is known Hindemith created his drama.

Grünewald was court painter to the Archbishop Uriel von Gemmingen from 1508 to 1514 and after that date until 1526 to the Archbishop Albrecht von Brandenburg. He painted the famous *Isenheim Altar* sometime before 1516. It is not surprising that he became involved in the controversies of the Reformation, when one considers that the court he served stood at the very center of that movement. That he leaned towards the teachings of Luther, as did Dürer, is apparent from the fact that the New Testament, and many sermons and pamphlets by Luther, appeared as items of his estate when it was listed.

The opera is based on the incident of Grünewald's leaving his workshop in Selingenstadt and his office at the court of Mainz in 1525 to join the Peasants' War against the nobles. When the Archbishop recaptured Selingenstadt the painter fled to Frankfurt, and although he was acquitted, he refused to return to his patron's service. The opera has him turn to the construction of water mills, refusing ever to touch paint to canvas again.

The symphony is based on music taken from the central episode of the opera. As night falls in the forest into which Matthias has fled, his great pictures come to life before his eyes and merge with the historical characters of the drama. From this material which served as the background for the tableaux, the composer created a concert work that is in no way program music, in no way picturesque, but essentially classical in design. In other words, this is a piece of music to be understood in purely musical terms and yet one that was inspired by painting.

The three movements of Hindemith's symphony are the "Angelic Concert," the "Entombment," and the "Temptation of St. Anthony." We know therefore the exact panels of the *Isenheim Altar* to which the composer referred. Let us turn therefore to the paintings and examine their salient features.

The *Isenheim Altar* was ordered by the abbot Guido Guersi for the monastery church of St. Anthony in Isenheim. We cannot fail to be impressed immediately by the cruel treatment of Christ's suffering. He is covered with open sores and the suggestion has been made by scholars that this painting was intended for a hospital and reflected the dreadful plague of syphilis that was sweeping over Europe at that time. The contrast between the human

Figure 1. The *Isenheim Altar*, outer wings closed: central panel, *Crucifixion*; predella, *Entombment*.

and the saintly is apparent in the figures of this painting (Fig. 1). Arthur Burkhard points out that

> Nearest Christ . . . kneels the comparatively small form of the Magdalene, with her hands in a clasp of anguish upraised toward Him, a symbol of agonized despair. [In contrast, the figure of the Virgin Mary is] distant, heroic, tragic, and contained. . . . The Virgin's mantle is white and cold, her form is rigid and firm, her face lifeless, her eyes closed.[6]

St. Sebastian stands firmly on the right pointing to Christ to emphasize the meaning to man of Christ's crucifixion. The human is emphasized by the kneeling figure of Mary Magdalene. The predella pictures the Entombment. As the wings are opened to reveal other pictures of other moods, this predella always remains to remind us of Christ's death. It is this small panel that serves as the inspiration for the middle movement of Hindemith's symphony.

As we open the wings to the central panel of this altarpiece we are introduced to a brighter mood. "The composition," to quote Burkhard again

> seems to spring not so much from the brain of the creator as from his imaginative vision. His expressionistic art seeks to convey in sensuous terms the visionary and supernatural, the incommensurable and transcendental, that which the eye cannot see nor the reason grasp. . . . The figures in these moving, dynamic, metaphysical paintings, which are revelations of the invisible realm of the spirit, very appropriately appear as worlds in themselves with their own laws of equilibrium and their own peculiar principles of proportion. . . . The comprehensive treatment of the three pictures . . . as a single unit becomes apparent on careful inspection. The heavy figures of the dark *Annunciation* [on the left] pull the eye down to earth [the word of God becomes human] (Fig. 2); the ethereal figure of Christ in the *Resurrection* [on the right] radiantly bright, draws the eye upward toward heaven[7] (Fig. 3).

The middle panel, the *Incarnation*, is divided into two sections: the *Celestial Choir* on the left and *Joys of the Virgin* on the right. *Celestial Choir* is the inspiration for the first movement of Hin-

Figure 2. The *Isenheim Altar,* left outer wing, interior: *Annunciation.*

Figure 3. The *Isenheim Altar,* right outer wing, interior: *Resurrection.*

demith's symphony. In this panel, as in the *Crucifixion*, both the heavenly and the earthly are present (Fig. 4).

> The mystic and supernatural elements are nowhere too much stressed. On the contrary, the figures of the foreground are definitely of this earth. . . . To the left of the crib stands prominently displayed an oval wooden tub, covered with a towel for the bath; beside it to the right, the *vaso di notte*—unmistakable, if somewhat naively proffered, evidence that in this child God has become man.[8]

When we open the inner wings to the final view of this altarpiece we find two panels: on the left the tranquil scene of *St. Anthony and St. Paul the Hermit* (Fig. 5) in conversation, on the right the *Temptation of St. Anthony* (Fig. 6). In this latter picture, which served Hindemith as the basis for his last movement, a grotesque battle between the forces of good and evil for the soul of man is portrayed. St. Anthony "tries to raise his thin voice above the tumult in a wail of lamentation. Nor does his shrill cry for help remain unheeded. God the Father, faintly visible enthroned on high, has dispatched the Archangel Michael to join combat with the devils, some of whom are already dropping like dead flies into the consuming flames."[9] The predella may have remained closed, since it does not open as a part of the upper wings, and our eyes at this moment may fall to the lamentation of the Entombment and we may think of the meaning for man of Christ's death.

The key to the central idea of Hindemith's symphony is to be found, I think, in the middle movement which is inspired by the predella. This painting, divided in the middle so that it, too, can open as wings to reveal the sculpture behind it, is from structural necessity in two parts. So that the line of division will not cut directly across the body of Christ, the main figures of the panel

Figure 4. The *Isenheim Altar*, outer wings open: central panel, *Incarnation. Celestial Choir* and *Joys of the Virgin.*

Figure 5. The *Isenheim Altar*, left inner wing, interior: *St. Anthony and St. Paul the Hermit* in conversation.

Figure 6. The *Isenheim Altar,* right inner wing, interior: *Temptation of St. Anthony.*

are collected on the right and form something of a unit picturing death. The left panel of the predella is unified by a vista into a sunlit region which lies mostly beyond a dark river.

This spot is the brightest in the entire panel and one's eye immediately seeks it. From here we travel along the parallel lines of the tomb to the figures on the right, changing our mood perhaps as we sense the anguish on the face of the earthly figure of Mary Magdalene as she gazes at the dead Christ. When we come to the right-hand panel our eye finds the stability of a circular pattern and we rest upon this calm scene of death.

The second movement of Hindemith's symphony obviously reflects the general mood of the picture of the Entombment. The music has calm dignity: a funeral pace that is without pathos. The piece is written in two-part structure and follows very closely the sectional divisions of the panel. The first part has far less stability than the second. Almost immediately the ear is led into a transitional movement just as the eye is led from the sunlit scene to the figures beside the dark tomb. But the methods that the composer has used to bring about this sense of movement are entirely different. A translation has been made into musical devices that can reveal to us both the way in which the composer works and a curious symbolism.

The slow movement starts with a very strong focus of the music on the tonal level of C–natural, a key that musicians consider bright. And yet the very first phrase of the music starts to move away from this level into the more shadowy tonality of sharps. The orchestration also contributes to a sense of movement, for there is an antiphonal use of strings and woodwinds and a use of sudden dynamic changes that lead the ear along to the climax marking the end of the section. When this point is reached a simple chord is sounded indicating a new tonality.

The second section is completely stable on the tonality of C–sharp. There is no sense of movement. The mood of the music is one of calm and sorrow. Hindemith appears to have chosen this unique design consciously, for the reason that C–sharp is as far removed from C–natural as is acoustically possible. To have started on one tonal level and to have ended on a remote tonal level is very unusual in music. There seems no doubt that Hindemith chose this device to reflect in his music the symbolism of the painting, for the transition from life to death is the greatest that man knows. We have a clue, therefore, that may be significant as we examine the entire symphony. C–natural has been associated with life, with the earthly, and C–sharp with death and the spiritual.

I do not make the point that it is necessary to understand this symbolism in order to understand the music. My point is this: we have seen how a composer has translated an external idea into musical architecture. We have perhaps also peered into the mind of the composer to see his attitude towards the mystery of sound. We have seen that the composer's handling of the levels of pitch in his music is by no means haphazard, though I must add that rarely will such symbolism as we have found here be so apparent.

When we listen to this music, our main impression will be, I am sure, that of a journey—a transition. The thematic material itself has the quality of a slow stride, dignified and deep in sorrow.

Now we turn to the first movement of the symphony, the "Angelic Concert." The vividness of the color in the painting matches the noisy sound of playing and singing, and also emphasizes the three-fold accent that characterizes this painting (Fig. 7). There are three levels of color: the lovely light color in the foreground, the vivid red in the middle, and the warm purple in the background. There are three angels performing on viols. Notice the pattern that their bows make and notice particularly the distortion of the bow-arm of the angel in the foreground, a distortion that accentuates the triangle of the instruments. There are three groups of performers: the instrumentalists, a choir with bright halos immediately behind, and far in the background an encircled choir (faintly visible in Fig. 4).

When we turn to the score we see immediately that this three-fold accent is carried out in the music. A slow introduction starting on the pitch level of G (the first overtone of C—standing symbolically for the earthly) introduces three buttresses of chords. Then is introduced the German folksong, "Es sungen drei Engel." This song has the quality of a Lutheran chorale and is introduced on the tonal level of D–flat. Although I hesitate to dwell upon the possible symbolism, I cannot refrain from pointing out that D–flat is between C–natural and C–sharp. Could this imply a sacred melody that is partly divine and partly human?

Figure 7. The *Isenheim Altar*, detail of the *Celestial Choir: The Angels' Serenade*.

However that may be, the tune is introduced fugally with three statements: the first in trombones, the second in horns, and the third in trumpets. Then, in punctuation, three chords mark the end of the introduction.

There follows the exposition of a sonata-allegro form. The first theme, a joyous one, starts with a solid foundation on G but moves to B. Then comes a transition which uses three chords in rapid succession. The first theme continues through D and E and finally returns to G, ending with three larger chord buttresses.

The second theme is also cheerful and is focused on the pitch level of F–sharp, which has strong relations both to G and C–sharp. A third theme rests more solidly on G and gives us the impression that the first section of the music is coming to an end, as it does on three chords rooted on B. Thus we have an exposition made up of three themes and largely circling around G or notes that have a close relation to G.

The tonal focus of the development is much less clear. Indeed the interest of the composer seems to be, as one might expect, in the complexity of the themes. He combines the first and second themes into an ingenious texture with a sense of gaiety. Suddenly in the middle of the development the folktune re-enters, again on the level of D–flat. Once more there is a three-voice fugal statement and around it continues the chatter of the development. The first theme returns but in a very different, much less happy, mood, this time focused not on G but on C–sharp. Perhaps this entrance foreshadows the tonal level of C–sharp that will arrive in the "Entombment" movement which follows. The second and third themes return. Indeed, all of the themes recur as the movement ends on the pitch level of G with three chords sounding loudly in the brass.

The last movement is based on the *Temptation of St. Anthony* and, like the painting, depicts a battle between the forces of good and evil, between the tonalities of C–natural and C–sharp. An attempt is made by the composer to match the grotesqueness and cruelty of the picture, but there is one striking difference. Hindemith has not only framed his music in a mood that belongs to the *Crucifixion,* but he has included a middle section referring, specifically I feel sure, to the *Entombment* which might be seen if one's eyes dropped to the predella. He has reflected, in other words, a broader range of feeling than Grünewald did in the single picture of St. Anthony's temptation.

I shall not dwell on the slow introduction to this last movement. Careful examination of this section reveals many curious thematic references, among which one becomes important later as an ostinato at the end of the symphony.

After the introduction the movement bursts out into a wild theme on C–sharp which rushes forward with little tonal stability. Three fortissimo chords end this theme and then an eerie second theme begins which centers on C–natural and G. One hears particularly the woodwinds playing in fourths, an effect that produces a weird sound.

There is a sudden hush and then a furious assault, a terrific struggle between C–natural and C–sharp coming to its climax on C–sharp only to be dissipated by a shimmering trill on C–natural high on the violins.

Beneath this high organ-point is introduced the reference back to the "Entombment," and just as in the slow movement, this slow section moves from C–natural to C–sharp. But there is one striking difference, one that I cannot explain. In the middle of this slow section the tonal point of B–flat is twice reached—a pitch level entirely new and entirely strange to the work. It is the point, perhaps, of greatest beauty in the whole composition and each time that I arrive there I am filled with awe.

At the very end of this section the tonal level of C–sharp is reached in the bass. In rapid succession the three themes of this movement are reintroduced, but in reverse order, and one has the feeling that the battle weakens.

Suddenly the battle stops and we move into a coda that is perhaps Hindemith's comment on the whole work. After a relaxed beginning this coda suddenly introduces a musical wheel—an ostinato taken from the introduction—that goes round and round, never leaving the pitch level of its axis of A–flat which prepares the final pitch level of D–flat. Suddenly a medieval hymn, a fragment of a plainsong, is introduced above this wheel leading to the highest dynamic climax of the piece.

The work ends on a jubilant and brassy "Alleluia" establishing the level of D–flat, the level of the chorale in the first movement. Perhaps by such hymns of praise might man solve the struggle between the human and the divine. The tonal struggle between C–natural and C–sharp ends on the compromise of D–flat.

We find in *Matthias the Painter* a symbolism in the relationship of pitch levels to ideas, a type of symbolism not uncommon in poetry or painting but little understood in music. For several hundred years composers in Western culture have felt that pitch levels—key levels—have had specific meaning. The physicist assures us that such symbolic associations cannot be true, but the artist, with his sensitive ears, keeps right on believing that they are. Hindemith writes of "acoustic phenomena as a mirror of the life of the spirit. . . ."[10] Intervals [speak] . . . of the first days of the creation of the world: mysterious as Number, of the same stuff as the basic concepts of time and space, the very dimensions of the audible as of the visible world, building stones of the universe. . . ."[11] Let us not enter into this argument, for it is not germane to our purpose. Whatever the truth, there is no question whatsoever as to Hindemith's beliefs.

In 1948 Hindemith published a revision of his earlier song cycle, *The Life of Mary (Das Marienleben)*, written to poetry by Rainer Maria Rilke. In the preface to this edition Hindemith expressed his conviction that there can be symbolic meaning in tone relations. He wrote:

> On the basis of the old equation that key equals feeling or expression: Let a fixed emotional region of the hearer be symbolized by a fixed key. . . . I can go even further yet and instead of the equation that Tonality equals the condition of feeling, expand it so that Tonality will equal the intellectual grouping of ideas in order enormously to expand the field of tonal symbolism.[12]

Hindemith admits that such a symbolic planning of tonality, based as it is on the will of the composer, undermines the stable appearance of tonal organization that previously was trusted, but he points out that artistic freedom is necessarily limited by a thorough understanding of the principles of tonal organization. On the basis of such a symbolic plan, he explains the meanings that he associates in *Marienleben* with specific levels. Very freely generalized they are as follows: E is the symbol for the spirituality of Christ. The dominant B symbolizes the Virgin Mary and therefore the earthly relation of Christ. The subdominant A stands for the relation of Christ to heavenly forces. C symbolizes the infinite, the universe. C–sharp or D–flat stands for the inevitable; D symbolizes trust. E–flat stands for the greatest purity, the most sublime, and finally, death. F symbolizes, in its unique relationship to E and B, whatever urges us to pity; F–sharp stands for the smallness of man in comparison to the heavenly. G symbolizes the idyllic—particularly in the lowly house of Joseph. G–sharp stands for our incapacity to understand the miraculous.

We found my symbolism in *Matthias the Painter* to translate ideas present in visual art. In *Marienleben*, there is no such translation. Symbolism is developed as a purely musical craft. This craft does not stand in the way of musical expression; indeed, it is not particularly necessary that one understand the symbolism in order to respond to the music. The symbolism may interest us, but it is not for this reason that I have brought it to attention. My object has been to show that from whatever source the inspiration of the composer may come, a translation into abstract musical values must take place.

Hindemith, like many recent composers, reveals a profound concern with an absolute formal design that stands not in opposition to expression as the Romantic might contend, but that, in ordering thought, becomes expression. The modern artist believes, with Stravinsky, that "the creator's function is to sift the elements he receives, . . . for human activity must impose limits upon itself. The more art is controlled, limited, worked over, the more it is free."[13]

Or, to quote T. S. Eliot, to seek an expression

> (where every word is at home,
> Taking its place to support the others,
> The word neither diffident nor ostentatious,
> An easy commerce of the old and the new,
> The common word exact without vulgarity,
> The formal word precise but not pedantic,
> The complete consort dancing together).[14]

(1951)

3

The Value of the Abstract

In 1956 the great English composer Ralph Vaughan Williams visited the University of Michigan where I was composer-in-residence, and a student from the *Michigan Daily* asked to have an interview for his paper. He arrived at my home with photographer and proceeded to ask questions. Vaughan Williams had just turned eighty-four. He was a lovable man, a little deaf, and his old-fashioned ear-trumpet and his beetle brow made him look like a grumpy character out of a Trollope novel.

When his picture appeared next day on the front page, underneath was the caption: "Composer Says Music Isn't Worth Anything." I was taken aback when I read this caption for it distorted so completely Vaughan Williams's meaning. He had said that the values of music were not materialistic, that music could not and should not be valued in dollars and cents. But in making such a statement he implied, of course, that music had a very different value, none the less real for being unmeasurable in everyday currency. Probably the newspaper statement shows that people are quite sure that music is worth something, and to have a composer say that it isn't is shocking.

This episode started a train of thought. Undoubtedly it was possible for the newspaper to shock its readers with the statement that music isn't worth anything because people accept completely and without question the value of music. There are values that one doesn't have to defend because they are fundamentally a part of human culture. Yet we are not quite sure of the place of music in our lives, and over the centuries the question of music's worth has been asked and answered many times.

John Locke asked himself the question when he had *Some Thoughts concerning Education*. After having stated his qualified approval of dancing, he writes:

> Music is thought to have some affinity with dancing, and a good hand, upon some instruments, is by many people mightily valued. But it wastes so much of a young man's time, to gain but a moderate skill in it, and engages often in such odd company, that many think it much better spared; and I have, amongst men of parts and business, so seldom heard any one commended or esteemed for having an excellency in music, that amongst all those things, that ever came into the list of accomplishments, I think I may give it the last place.[1]

It is perhaps pertinent to mention that John Locke doesn't advise painting, either, because ". . . ill painting is one of the worst things in the world; and to attain a tolerable degree of skill in it requires too much of a man's time."[2] Locke looked upon music as a recreational skill, and he did not distinguish clearly between that skill and the creative act of painting. He implied that the creative aspect of the arts concerns only the specially trained, and that the young gentleman is concerned with the arts only in so far as they may supply relaxation and social prestige.

Locke's view was much narrower than the ideas about music that St. Augustine expressed in the fourth century. The classic ideas of Plato and Plotinus were reflected in the writings of that theologian. He had no interest in music as entertainment, but expounded the power of music to influence deeply people's lives. He delved into the many facets of musical perception and understanding, and it is not difficult to translate his ideas into modern terminology, for he anticipates much of our psychological and physiological thinking about music. He suggests degrees or steps in the musical experience, which I can best describe by quoting Paul Hindemith's paraphrase.

> First, there is the mere physical fact of sound. Although sound can exist independent of any listener, it is indispensable as a basic experience before the perception and mental absorption of music can take place. Second, there is our faculty of hearing: the physiological fact that sound waves act upon our ear and by muscular and nervous transmission release reactions in the brain's center of hearing.[3]

His third and fourth points deal with the capacity of man to imagine music mentally, without its actually being sounded, and to remember past performances of music and their associations.

With the fifth point, he comes to the idea of the intellect's examining and judging musical shape and quality. "Thus the mere activity of perceiving or imagining music is combined with the satisfaction we derive from classifying and evaluating it. But we must not become slaves of this enjoyable satisfaction; . . . Musical order, as recognized and evaluated by our mind, is not an end in itself."[4]

St. Augustine has traveled from the simple concepts of sound to the idea of intellectual participation in the musical experience. He has developed the concept of music as a language, and from this point he steps off into the classical idea of metaphysical music. "It is an image of a higher order which we are permitted to perceive if we proceed one step further to the sixth degree on our scale of musical assimilation: if we put our enjoyment of such knowledge . . . into the side of the balance that tends towards the order of the heavens and towards the unification of our soul with the divine principle."[5]

Locke, the rationalist of the late seventeenth and eighteenth centuries, limited his interest to those qualities of music that were obvious and easily proved. When he ventured into a discussion of metaphysical music he repeated ancient beliefs with little conviction. This viewpoint led him to consider the physical properties of sound and the physiological process of hearing. It was natural that he should be conscious of the sensuous pleasure of music and give emphasis to virtuosity in performance. The ancient concern with metaphysical music which had led to speculation concerning the psychology of music as a language was neglected.

Now, if music's worth is merely a matter of a polite accomplishment, as Locke thought, it should indeed be given little place in the education of men. The young gentleman of the seventeenth century may have thought that he had little time, but how much more crowded is the life of a student today. If music, like dancing, merely improves physical co-ordination, there are surely available exercises that take less time and do a better job. (As a musician, I am forced to ignore Locke's remark about "odd company.")

The realm of metaphysical music, however, still haunts us. It is reflected in our interest in musical therapy. In our mental hospitals, music is used to help treat psychological disturbances. It is found that music brings response where every other means of communication fails. Music is somehow related to the factor of human fatigue. The idea that by perceiving the balance and unity of art we can gain a balance and unity in life is never quite abandoned.

Does art hold some mystery, some secret, that can somehow put our lives in tune with a universal order? Certainly no scientific experiment has proved that music has any such power, but we no longer hold with Shakespeare's idea that

> . . . this muddy vesture of decay
> Doth grossly close (us) in,[6]

or that some mysterious quality known to the Greeks is no longer valid for us. If art did have this power to bring order to people's lives, an order based on perceiving order in art, art would indeed be one of the most valuable factors in social adjustment. We, however, turn to psychological rather than to metaphysical explanations, not quite willing to abandon old beliefs, but certain that understanding must come from the study of man's behavior.

Modern philosophers, concerned with psychology and anthropology, have sought to understand the value of the arts in terms of communication. There are many schools of aesthetics, but all accept the idea that "art is an independent 'universe of discourse'."[7] In other words, whatever attributes of play—of recreation—the arts may have, their unique quality is the symbolic language they constitute. We come to understand that the arts are not more creative than many other human endeavors, but that their creative quality is different.

Ernst Cassirer perhaps expressed this difference in creativity when he said that "science gives us order in thoughts; morality gives us order in actions; art gives us order in the apprehension of visible, tangible, and audible appearances."[8] Art may be defined as symbolic language, and music is the symbolic language of emotional gesture.

Music is not the language of emotion in the sense that it reflects the personal and individual emotions of the composer. The everyday feelings of a composer are not expressed in his music. On the other hand, we must not fall into the error of assuming that music has no emotional meaning.

Roger Sessions describes this power. Music, he says,

communicates the attitudes inherent in, and implied by, . . . movement; its speed, its energy, its élan or impulse, its tenseness or relaxation, its agitation or its tranquility, its decisiveness or its hesitation. It communicates in a marvelously vivid and exact way the dynamics and the abstract qualities of emotion. . . . Each musical phrase is a unique gesture and through the cumulative effect of such gestures we gain a clear sense of a quality of feeling behind them. . . . Music . . . develops and moves on a level that is essentially below the level of conscious emotion. Its realm is that of emotional energy rather than that of emotion in the specific sense.[9]

Cassirer points out that there is

an unmistakable difference between the symbols of art and the linguistic terms of ordinary speech or writing. These two activities agree neither in character nor purpose; they do not employ the same means, nor do they tend toward the same ends. Neither language nor art gives us mere imitation of things or actions; both are representations. But a representation in the medium of sensuous forms differs widely from a verbal or conceptual representation.[10]

There is nothing truly comparable in music to the precise meaning of words. It is, of course, true that poetry is less dominated by the precise meaning of words than is discourse. If one tries to define the precise word meaning of Blake's poem,

> Tiger! Tiger! burning bright
> In the forests of the night[11]

one ends up with nonsense. We know what a tiger is, but how does a tiger burn? Obviously, poetry demands something more from us than the analysis of precise word meaning: it demands an understanding of symbolic meaning. For this reason one would never dream of teaching poetry in the same way that one would teach discourse.

Music is infinitely less precise in meaning than is poetry. But the exact manner in which the gesture is articulated is very precise in music. No two people can expect to have a similar emotional reaction to a given piece of music, but they will be able to agree on those qualities of tempo and dynamics and pitch definition that are so strictly controlled by the composer. Because of this difference, musical form is a much more fluid organization than even the most subtle verbal form. The precision of meaning in verbal form holds the structure together. It is the precision of tempo and dynamics and pitch that holds the musical structure together, and this structure is held in memory at the same time that one gives oneself over to the flow of movement.

It seems obvious that no single language can express the whole man and that to think of verbal discourse as the only form of human communication is to distort and narrow human capacity. The seventeenth-century philosopher spoke of outer and inner senses, making a difference, I judge, between the stimulation of the sensory organ and the ordering of that stimulation within the mind so that it becomes a communication.

Lewis Mumford has written: "Starting as an animal among the

animals, man has stretched and intensified certain special organic capacities in order to develop more fully what is specifically human."[12] It is not necessary to argue the importance of language to the human being—without language man would not be human; but it is important to point out that the language of discourse is but one part of human communication, and that the arts form another very important part. Only by keeping in mind the multiplicity of human expression can music and the arts be understood as a basic part of education.

This multiplicity is apparent in that enchanting period of infancy when the child seeks expression by babbling. During this uniquely human period of development, as Susanne Langer has pointed out, the child experiments with all the means of human communication.[13] To his parents' distress, he learns to distinguish between high and low sounds, between loud and soft sounds, between regular and irregular meter—indeed, all of the stuff of musical language. He learns the relationships of things in space and the contrasts of color that often define such relationships. He may even learn those simple relationships of number that eventually he will use to describe abstract form. The parent tries to ignore these early adventures into language until the child makes the association of sound and object and the language of discourse is begun. At this point the parent recognizes what the child is up to and becomes almost ridiculous in his efforts to forward the experiments in verbal communication. But the other phases of expression often are neglected.

The most important period for the cultivation of human communication is this early phase of babbling. Here is the great moment for music education. I am often amused to find that the teacher of music education, as defined by most of our schools of music, is that individual who teaches music to children ranging in age from about six to seventeen. The college teacher is not a music educator for some reason or other, and nobody, not even the doting parent, will concern himself with the musical education of the babbling child. But what a great pity! For immediately begins the neglect that leads to the imbalance of our inner senses, an imbalance that can be overcome somewhat in later years, but that need not have existed in the first place.

There is recognized tragedy in a person who lacks human senses, but we judge this lack largely from an external, physiological standpoint. To be blind or deaf or mute we recognize as having important effects upon the human personality. We do not consider the lack of inner senses as tragic, and yet is the psychologist sure that such imbalance does not contribute to personal maladjustment?

I am not so sure that the lack of outer senses is any more tragic than the lack of inner senses. I have known blind people infinitely more balanced in their inner language senses—in their capacity to listen to music and to understand poetry or the abstract symbols of mathematics or even the spatial organization of sculpture—than others who were neither deaf, dumb, nor blind. The lack of the sensory organ is, of course, a great handicap, but the incapacity to use that organ in conjunction with the mind is an equal handicap.

Modern psychology seems to accept, in large part, the view that I have expressed of art as language, and there is growing recognition of the importance of the child's earliest sensory experiences. In other words, Locke's rationalism is not so very rational in the twentieth century. Indeed, it seems to me incredibly narrow, and the aesthetics that views art merely as recreation has contributed to a neglect that may be responsible for many personal imbalances. It seems valid to re-examine the whole process of musical education, keeping in mind the fact that we will not find the greatest values in recreation but in experiencing and understanding the creative language of the art, in the symbolic manner in which music mirrors emotional gesture.

Children are born with different sensory capacities, related, undoubtedly, to differences in their organs of sense; but these differences should be minimized rather than exaggerated. Most people are born with reasonably good vision and hearing, adequate enough to expect a reasonable development of linguistic skill. The idea that only the rare person has a capacity for verbal discourse is not commonly held. There is little talk of an aristocracy in the realm of speech.

But in music the idea seems commonplace that only the rarest individual possesses the capacity for musical language, and that indeed there is an aristocracy of the arts. I question whether there is a great difference between individuals' capacity to hear music. Certainly the composer, like the writer, must become a master of language and the performer must develop the greatest sensitiveness and control; but even though the composer creates the music and the performer gives utterance to that creation, the listener in following that utterance is not concerned with a musical experience essentially different. If there is an audience for music—and how can we doubt that there is—then the capacity to hear must not vary too greatly from person to person.

Roger Sessions points out that "the high degree of differentiation reached in the course of the development of music should not obscure the fact that in the last analysis composer and performer (and listener) are not only collaborators in a common enterprise but participants in an essentially single experience."[14] Differences in musical capacity are certainly apparent in the adolescent child, but these differences are more often the result of neglect and educational misunderstanding than of ill-formed eardrums. There is no reason to suppose that the child could not develop as naturally his capacity to understand musical gesture as he does his ability to understand all the abstract complexities of verbal discourse.

Indeed, the whole pattern of symbolic language, so essentially a part of human experience, could be developed in a natural way if it were not delayed until inhibitions and frustrations had already complicated the process. I am not so sure that adolescent difficulties in grappling with the problems of numbers and abstract form, with understanding music, with seeing spatial values, exist because of inadequate teaching in secondary schools. They may stem from the habit of viewing these skills as purely recreational, and of lesser importance than the skill of discourse.

However that may be, when we examine the place of the arts in the college curriculum, we see them as part of the whole fabric of human expression and communication rather than as recreational. We consider him well educated who has been able to develop into adulthood those elementary language capacities with which he was endowed as a babe. In education, we are concerned both with the development of the whole personality and with the development of special gifts. A student's special interest in abstract form may lead him into the realm of the scientist; his verbal skills may encourage him to activity as a historian or writer or lawyer; his enthusiasm for the representation of the world of space or the world of movement and time may lead him to be an artist. Thus he specializes. But the breadth of his education depends upon his awareness and understanding of all those areas in which man is creative.

The liberal arts view is not limited. It is a concept of education that has affected all of our institutions and is related, I think, to this matter of developing all of the symbolic language capacities that we have. In a literal sense the liberal arts curriculum is centered in the areas of human communication: religion, mathematics, verbal languages, art, and music.

From these languages concerned with the symbolic expression of abstract ideas fan out the many areas of creative achievement. Religion and philosophy direct our concern to moral principles. From mathematics one enters science, the search for order in the phenomena of the physical universe. From verbal languages spring not only our great literatures but all those disciplines that are concerned with historical and social questions. Art supplies all of the skills by which we make space significant: painting, sculpture, architecture, and the like. Music gives us an understanding of movement and a mirror of emotional action. All of these creative areas, so interrelated in primitive cultures, are fundamental parts of our liberal arts education.

The European tradition of education separated these creative areas. Music was developed in the conservatory except in so far as it touched historical discipline. The arts were taught in schools of design. Mathematics was sometimes relegated to the technical institute. The division had some merit since each area was given special support from the state, and it does not follow that a narrow education necessarily resulted from the separation. But the point I wish to make is that we, in the New World, have not followed the European pattern. Except in a few technical schools, our institutions—universities and colleges alike—shelter under the same roof all the creative disciplines. Composer rubs shoulders with physicist, mathematician with painter, poet with historian. A new idea of education has emerged, and a framework for carrying out that idea. But this confederation of man's human capacities will not succeed unless each discipline understands its function within the whole, and our understanding cannot be based upon ancient philosophy.

My concern is how music can be made a part of this broader concept of the liberal arts. It seems to me that only by re-examining the value of music can we come to a sound idea of its position in education. But before we do that, let us glance back at the way in which music started in our colleges.

The inclusion of the creative arts in the American college and university did not take place, as you might suppose, from a clear understanding of educational objectives. Even today, educators are a little bewildered by the pattern that has developed. It is so different from traditional European education. But I have no doubt that our organization within the college is here to stay. The natural scientist has made his place respected and secure. We have come to understand the necessity of laboratory techniques as a process of scientific education, and after the initial struggle during the past century, the college has come to accept creative work in science for what it is. It has recognized that the history of science is no substitute for experimental examination of man's natural environment. I have no doubt that in time the arts and the creative procedures of the arts will be similarly accepted and understood.

Most of our college music departments in this country, like Topsy, just "growed." From the beginning, there was no intention that musical study should be limited to historical scholarship as in foreign universities; indeed, quite the contrary. In an environment which struggled with the hardships of pioneer life, the arts expressed refinement. This yearning was real even if it was not genuinely understood. More often than not a local piano teacher who gave lessons to a few college students was allowed some loose connection with the institution in return for playing hymns in the chapel service. In time, this teacher was given a studio on the campus and allowed to teach on a pro-rata basis: that means that the college administration received adequate income to cover the costs of the studio, and the teacher was insured a large source of students. It would be my guess that the first courses in the history and theory of music were given, not because of administrative policy, but because of the enthusiasms of this early teacher and the surrounding student group.

That his musical insight was often narrow does not justify heaping scorn upon him at this late date. The early teacher often was ill-informed in matters of history and theory, and primarily concerned with the recreational aspect of music; but it was the recreational and prestige values of music for which pioneer society yearned. It was human nature for this music teacher to hold before his students the glamorous future of a concert career or at least a chance to impress the local community.

Nothing in his education made him at ease in the intellectual environment of the college, and he sought for self-realization not within the community but as a representative of a musical world that existed largely in his own imagination. Not infrequently he was "odd company," unorthodox in his social relations and hypnotized by a romantic concept of the arts long vanished.

Many departments of music grew by a process of addition. A voice teacher was added, a violin teacher—always on a pro-rata basis. There was no change of philosophy. Each teacher struggled to gain greater security by teaching more and more students. The music teacher continued to be considered something of a Bohemian, and professional frictions between music teachers were considered a necessary and slightly racy part of campus life. Nevertheless, a new educational pattern had been established. The arts may have entered the university by the back door, but they were there to stay.

The badly organized, badly administered music department that I have described is disappearing. The change is due to the fact that our administrators are becoming aware of the unique opportunity that the liberal arts curriculum offers. The music faculty, largely trained in American institutions that reflect our concepts of education, feels a part of the intellectual environment and is accepted as equal by its colleagues.

But the old ideas die hard. Music as a means of attaining social prestige and of showing off still controls much of the thinking of teachers and parents. To view music as a polite accomplishment encourages emphasis upon its performance-recreational side. It leads to all those distortions of display and virtuosity that Aristotle wrote about in the *Politics* when he condemned the teaching of the flute. He points out that it was good that Athene, after finding the flute, threw it away "out of annoyance because of the ugly distortion of her features." Aristotle continues that Athene probably acted as she did "because education in flute-playing has no effect on the intelligence."[15]

Now, this is perhaps a bit hard on the flute, but how often do young people learn to play an instrument in the college band, merely to put it away in mothballs for the rest of their lives. The experience has not contributed to development of their minds.

Aristotle argues that students would get from music what they should if they "did not go on toiling at the exercises that aim at professional competitions, nor the wonderful and elaborate performances which have now entered into the competitions and have passed from the competitions into education," and then comes right to the point by observing that they would be better off if they "only practised exercises . . . until they are able to enjoy beautiful tunes and rhythms."[16]

His emphasis is upon the power of music to communicate to our feelings, upon music as a "language." When the emphasis in college is too much upon performance and too little upon listening, there is danger that the effects will not last.

This overemphasis on performance also has resulted in an unfortunate reaction. Administrations, sensing the need for a more rigorous and contributive discipline, turn to the European tradition of music in the university to give greater weight to historical scholarship. This emphasis can be salutary, but unfortunately it recognizes the wrong discipline. Musical and historical disciplines are different, and just as science had to insist upon the recognition of laboratory experimentation as its proper discipline, so music and the other arts must insist upon methods of education that are based upon the special problems inherent in learning to understand and use a symbolic language. The history of the arts, like the history of science, is not made less important by recognizing its limitations.

Discipline in the arts is rooted in the unique manner in which each communicates. I have already pointed out that in poetry one must be concerned with the symbolic meanings of words. I think we all agree that literalness in verbal understanding has often hindered appreciation of poetry. In teaching expository writing, the exact meaning of words is the essential factor in formal organization; but in teaching poetry the abstract quality of language becomes more important, and formal organization is less dependent upon literal meaning. I have no doubt that the tendency of the parent to overemphasize literal meaning in the early period when the child is discovering verbal language contributes to the later problem of appreciating the symbolic meanings of words.

There is similar contrast of communication between photography or highly realistic painting, and abstract painting and design. The former constructs itself on the basis of literal visual association, while the latter employs abstract organization based upon the symbolic meaning of spatial shapes. Here again the parent can damage the child's natural development by overemphasizing realistic shapes and forms.

Even in mathematics, there is a dichotomy between the simple problems of addition and subtraction and the abstract concepts of forms. The layman jokes about the difficulty that the mathematician has in adding up his bank statement. One does not study mathematics to be able to count to one hundred; one studies to learn the abstract logic that inheres in numbers and in spatial concepts.

All of the mediums of communication differ. The exact meaning of words quite rightly forms the basic core of verbal exposition. Words, however, are inadequate to express mathematical concepts and as a result an independent discipline has evolved.

Words are most inadequate to express the abstract values of music and painting. When we discuss what music is all about—what it means—we must become involved with matters of movement in time, and consider qualities of tone and pitch. It is not an oversimplification to insist that the most important properties of music can be defined by such contrasts as slow and fast, loud and soft, high and low, because music is a language in which these qualities are precisely defined.

When we turn to the educational problem to suggest ways in which music can be better understood in the liberal arts tradition, we must keep in mind that music communicates its meaning in a manner entirely different from that of verbal discourse, and that the disciplines that achieve perfection in the one will not accomplish results in the other.

It is the job of the music department to help the maturing adult establish an inner response to the external sensory effect of sound. The teacher often is confronted by a person who has neglected and even misdirected his natural, primitive responses to music. The individual's capacity to listen, however, does not degenerate from lack of development; it awaits awakening. The challenge to the teacher, and to the student, is to open up a more natural response to musical gestures and to music's abstract language. Henry Adams writes of his sudden discovery that music could form a pattern in his mind and states that "he was one day surprised to notice that his mind followed the movement of a Sinfonie. He could not have been more astonished had he suddenly read a new language. Among the marvels of education, this was the most marvellous."[17]

The teacher must free the student from the domination of verbal habits before he can hope to follow the movement of a Sinfonie. He must help the student to hear how music evolves its own meaning. The fact that music once was bound to words does not mean that methods of understanding poetical form can help in understanding musical form. Musical forms are different, as I have pointed out, because they cannot fall back at any time on precise meaning. Only when music is combined with words can such a formal organization be established. The phrases of music, therefore, must be understood as gestures and not as sentences. They have the fluidity and the mobility of gestures, and the form that results is much more like dance than like a poem. The only method that can succeed is not to describe what has been done but to point it out as it happens.

The meaning of the word "musicianship" is the mastery of the abstract language of music. The layman cannot hope to gain complete mastery, but there is no essential difference between what he learns about music and what the professional musician learns. I am bitterly opposed to courses in general education in which are included a few lectures about music. You might as well have a few lectures about a foreign language. What will you gain? Once again verbal discourse pushes out musical meaning. Students will talk about "classical form," "atonal structure," "romantic color." I once read in a criticism the phrase "dodecaphonic pentatonicism." When I contemplate the musical experience, such phrases are meaningless. The essence of music—the way in which a composer has made time meaningful—must be heard, must be felt, must be understood, but not necessarily talked about.

It is much easier to explain the value of the abstract in mathematics than it is in music. One hardly needs to defend pure mathematics in an age that has seen the rapid advance in nuclear physics stemming from the abstract mathematical theories of Einstein. We know that none of the great achievements of science could have taken place without the mathematician. Since science deals with the natural universe, its discoveries often have great worth in dollars and cents.

Music has little such worth. It deals with inner human qualities, and it is worth no more than the value we put upon those qualities.

When Vaughan Williams said that music wasn't worth anything, he meant that the values that have sometimes been ascribed to it in the past were not the most real values. To play the piano is not as good exercise as a nice long walk in the beautiful countryside. But to learn from playing the piano, or singing in the choir, or taking a course, that music expresses something of the human spirit that nothing else can express so well, and to acquire this sensitiveness for one's entire life: that is our objective. As we come to value the abstract, we develop our human senses.

(1957)

4

Education and the Creative Imagination in Music

Our concern with the problems of creative imagination is important because we know too little about this aspect of human culture, and yet we cannot ignore its importance in the educational process. I think there is general agreement that you can teach the artist the craft of his art, but you can't supply him with genius.

At the start we should distinguish the various phases of creative thought: the period of investigation, the period of blankness when there seem to be no ideas at all, the flash of inspiration, and then the long period of integrating experiences into a new concept or work. Most creative work, whether in science or art, follows some such pattern, although not necessarily in the order named and obviously not in the same way for every individual. Each episode deserves respect and understanding as a part of the creative process. The flash of inspiration is the most sensational, but inspiration does not always result in creative work. The period of blankness is hard to endure, but it may be most important in clearing the mind. And surely the process that Sinclair Lewis referred to as the "application of the seat of the pants to the seat of the chair,"[1] though not at all romantic, is equally important to all creative work.

The parent and the teacher can do much to stimulate creative behavior, but neither parent nor teacher can predict the pattern of genes that results in creativity. Even the artist must accept his innate gift as it is, and proceed from there to make the most that he can of it.

However, to make the most of a student's gift still leaves considerable latitude for teaching, and brings one quickly to the realization that curriculums are inadequate. While courses may deal adequately with facts, they may as easily stifle as encourage imagination. For this reason it is well for the university to stop every now and then and ask itself what it is doing to encourage this most individual part of a student's growth.

First, it is important to understand the different types of creativity in the many areas of man's culture, with the object of improving educational methods. It is obvious that creativity and imagination are as essential, and contribute as much, in one area as in another. The university is by tradition the gathering place for creative minds, and over the years it has proved itself fairly successful in dealing with this all-important aspect of human culture.

It is human frailty that has sometimes limited the vision of universities. When the techniques of history tended in the nineteenth century to limit creative methods in science, and in the twentieth century, creative methods in the arts, the university was not so much at fault as were the limitations of insight within university faculties. Particularly at a time when group activity is given such emphasis, it is encouraging for faculties to discuss the value of creative imagination in their various fields.

I never have found a more cogent discussion of man's capacities than that given by Ernst Cassirer in *An Essay on Man*. It is impossible to summarize his discussion in a few quotations, but perhaps one can highlight the differences between imagination in the arts and in science. Cassirer points out that "science gives us order in thoughts; . . . art gives us order in the apprehension of visible, tangible, and audible appearances."[2] He states further that

when the scientist describes an object he characterizes it by a set of numbers, by its physical and chemical constants. Art has not only a different aim but a different object. . . . Our aesthetic perception exhibits a much greater variety and belongs to a much more complex order than our ordinary sense perception. . . . Aesthetic experience . . . is pregnant with infinite possibilities which remain unrealized in ordinary sense experience. In the work of the artist these possibilities become actualities; they are brought into the open and take on a definite shape. . . . The imagination of the artist does not arbitrarily invent the forms of things. It shows us these forms in their true shape, making them visible and recognizable. The artist chooses a certain aspect of reality, but this process of selection is at the same time a process of objectification. . . . Once reality has been disclosed to us in this particular way, we continue to see it in this shape.[3]

These remarks of Cassirer, taken out of context, perhaps are an oversimplification, but they do point to the essential characteristics of creative imagination in the arts. The artist must deal with his subjective reaction to reality, and of necessity he must be emotionally involved with the experience to which he seeks to give concrete shape. However the composer may verbalize or symbolize, his music must be a subjective experience revealed entirely through musical sound. A creative statement in music is neither entirely expression nor entirely invention; it is a combination of them. One without the other is uncreative and unimaginative. Even though the composer may reduce the order of musical notes to a numerical formula, this formula cannot explain the essential subjective revelation that makes of the musical notes a work of art.

The matter of emotional involvement or identification seems to me worth examining. It is obvious that all creative people are deeply involved in their work. The question is, what pattern does that involvement take? The view has been held that a composer's music is a literal reflection of his emotional life: that he composes a love song only when he is in love and a lament when he is bereaved. If one thinks of the changing emotional gestures in a single piece of music, one realizes immediately how invalid this idea is; nevertheless it persists and is partly responsible for ignorance about the arts in academic circles.

There is another view to which I must admit I cannot subscribe: that music has no emotional meaning at all. This opposite extreme views the creative process as mechanical. Surely the truth lies between these two.

The composer does not project his personal emotional experiences so much as he does the patterns and shapes of general emotional experience—the substratum of feeling. He evolves a symbolic "language" that is a semblance of emotion. Whatever logic he employs to integrate his musical material, in the end this material must find emotional as well as intellectual response. So, while it is not true that the composer reflects his emotional life in his music, it is true that he must be emotionally involved in writing it. It is this emotional involvement that seems to me characteristic of creative imagination in the arts.

Now, does this emotional involvement or identity differ from creative imagination in science or history? I think it does, though I am aware that both scientist and historian experience a type of emotional involvement in their work. Perhaps I can make the difference clear by a personal reference.

I get very excited when I compose music, and I used to keep the coffee pot constantly at hand and frequently paced the floor. One day I asked myself what good this coffee break was doing and I realized that while I was relieving personal tensions, this emotional excitement would have no effect on an audience hearing my music. I was emotionally involved with the experience of working, but I was actually escaping from the emotional involvement of my music.

There is, in other words, a difference between being emotionally excited about working and emotionally involved in the music one is composing. While I would be loath to generalize, it seems to me possible that the scientist is as emotionally excited about his work as the artist, but that he is trained to avoid emotional involvement lest it destroy the accuracy of his observation, or the logic of his thought.

Archibald MacLeish once made the point that

"objectivity" is one of the *good* words of our contemporary vocabulary. Scientists are objective about their findings. . . . The word raises a standard to which our scientifically minded generation can repair as the men of the Nineties repaired to "passion" and the men of the Eighteenth Century to "sensibility." . . . It connotes a quality—a suppression of personal commitment and personal feeling—which is admirable in a journalist reporting the news or a scientist observing an experiment or a judge judging a case, but which is anything but admirable when there is a cause to defend or a battle to be fought.[4]

Objectivity is meaningless to the artist since the very substance of his work is subjective.

If there is a difference between art and science in the question of emotional involvement, then it follows that the environment for the artist's work will differ. Indeed, except for the obvious differences of technique, this difference in emotional involvement seems the most fundamental. Insight into the problems of creative imagination could be gained by studying the demands that each discipline makes upon the emotional system of the individual.

One can trace in Beethoven's sketches the way in which he became emotionally involved in the great theme of the last movement of the A–minor Quartet. It is a common experience when teaching young composers to find that notes have been written without the slightest emotional involvement. But I cannot imagine a scientist's complaining because his student felt no emotional involvement in his experiment.

To speak of the psychology of emotional involvement in art is beyond my capacity, but I should like to suggest a few points at which this matter seems to me to touch upon the educational problem.

The musical experience is basically similar whether one is composing, performing, or listening. All three experiences may or may not be creative. If the emotional involvement is in the activity alone, then the experience is purely recreational. The arts have a very high recreational value—a value not to be minimized, but also not to be confused with creative activity. Creative activity, as I have pointed out, demands both intellectual and emotional involvement—not the emotional involvement of doing, but a genuine identification with the patterns and meanings of the musical gesture.

The listener often fails to identify himself with the emotional gestures of the music, and he barely hears the devices that make up the gesture. He is swept along on the current of the music and excited by the recreational experience. The performer in a chorus or an orchestra may follow the creative direction of a conductor without himself gaining more than a recreational experience. We have all heard musical performances that have lacked emotional involvement, and on these occasions we willingly accept the word "play" in relation to the performance. Yet we have also heard performances that in their revelation of the music have been truly creative. Let us not automatically accept participation in musical group experiences as the development of creative imagination. Such development is much more likely to take place individually than in a group.

We are also likely to think that creative imagination develops later in one's educational experience. Certainly in music the most important development takes place in the babbling age of childhood, between two and four. At this age children often find their creative imaginations frustrated by lack of parental understanding. We exaggerate verbal learning at this early age and neglect the child's experiments with pitch and time and space—the substances of other human expressions. The parent is annoyed by childish experiments in loud and soft and high and low (the very substance of music), but when the child says "mama" or "papa"—when the first verbal association is made—the parent is delighted. Many a child has been so conditioned before he starts school that he believes that musical "language" is somehow naughty or funny, and not infrequently the whole musical training in school is built upon this flimsy foundation. The child is able to verbalize about art and perhaps even get excited about the recreational activity of doing, but he has built up restraints that prevent his becoming emotionally involved in the language of music.

Confusion in this matter of environment may also lead to misunderstanding and false evaluation of the creative artist. I mentioned earlier that the old fallacy that music was a reflection of the composer's emotional life dies slowly. The result is a criticism of the academic environment as a proper one for the composer. How can the college professor know anything about life?

More dangerous is the Bohemian tradition that this fallacy encourages among students and faculty. The Bohemian always confuses personal experience with creative emotional involvement in art. This confusion leads inevitably to insincerity and superficiality, and people often fail to distinguish between this undisciplined, uninvolved Bohemianism and the courageous independence of the real artist. The creative artist is as sensitive to such distortion of aesthetic values and as able to judge a student's work on these terms as the scientist is sensitive to distortion of fact.

As a reaction against the superficiality of Bohemianism in art, the theorist may deny entirely the necessity of emotional involvement in the learning of craft. It is not uncommon to hear the argument that theoretical study should be founded on the concept of noninvolvement. The idea seems to be that the creative person can turn his creativity on and off. Even if it were convenient to be free from the questions that a creative student asks, can we be sure that after we have denied the student the opportunity of emotional involvement in the learning of his craft he will suddenly change when confronting the mature expressive experience?

There is even a tendency to eliminate theory as a part of certain curriculums. If you are to teach music to children, do you need to know how to analyze or write music? It is in the study of the theory of music, whether taught by performer, composer, or theory teacher, that the student gains insight into the logic and order of the creative musical gesture. Without this insight his capacity may be limited to the recreational experience. Having denied the baby his normal experiment with musical language, having discouraged in adolescent years a creative study of musical substance, we then expect, too late, creative imagination in maturity.

An administrator of a fine scientific institution once bewailed in my presence the fact that the chemist, to take one example, lost the creative enthusiasm of his adolescent days during his undergraduate studies, and at the time in his doctoral work when such imagination was most needed, it seemed no longer to be there. Is it possible that studies which offer no outlet for creative imagination dull the student's vision and prepare him poorly for mature contribution? However that may be, I am sure that no curriculum in music which denies the student the experience of emotional involvement in the learning of craft will succeed in stimulating creative imagination.

In conclusion, I should like to point out that the encouragement of the artist on the university faculty also depends upon our recognition of the demands that emotional involvement makes upon his work. Any activity, whether academic or not, is dangerous to the artist if it interferes with the continuity of his thought. Anything that hinders emotional involvement in his work destroys inspiration. The artist thinks on two levels: one conscious, the other subconscious. His conscious thought may often be directed into the various activities of teaching not only without damage to his creative work but often stimulating it. His subconscious thought, however, cannot be diverted from his work without shattering the continuity of his creative activity.

It seems to me that it is the artist's subconscious mind that becomes emotionally involved with his expression and allows him to return day after day to the continuation of the emotional gestures in his music. The composer can survive in the university (provided that he has time to work) as long as he can protect the continuity of his thought below the conscious level. Other emotional strains, therefore, are unusually disturbing.

I am not talking about the psychological complex of his personality with which he has come to live more or less successfully. All creative people have personal problems that arise from their psychological adjustment. What disturbs him are the tensions that clutter his mind at night. Artists have a way of magnifying these tensions, and temperamental outbursts are a usual device for throwing them off. These tensions interrupt the continuity of the artist's work because they interrupt his capacity to be emotionally involved in his work. He may have the time to work and still feel the lack of involvement. I am convinced that what has been interrupted is subconscious thought. It is my belief that the conscious mind of the artist can throw off a certain amount of emotional tension and protect subconscious thought. When tensions or activities become so oppressive that the conscious mind cannot protect the subconscious, then the artist's creative work is placed in jeopardy.

Many of the eccentricities of the artist come from an instinctive effort to protect his capacity to react to his work. Inactivity, or "laziness" to the layman, may be the only way to repair damage that has been done by emotional strain. If his colleagues understood this process of work, would not the artist be freed from activities and routines that are so injurious to his creative life? Surely the artist's contribution to general college affairs is slight in comparison to his creative contribution.

The artist is no more in need of time to work than the scientist, nor is the scientist as an individual free from personal emotional strains. Indeed, I am certain that creative inspiration comes as mysteriously from the subconscious mind in scientists as it does in artists.

But does continuity of work in science come as much from subconscious thought as it does in art? Isn't the artist who deals with perception on such a subjective level more at the mercy of his emotional condition than the scientist or historian who deals with more objective facts?

Artists are relative newcomers to the university faculty. If their creative imaginations are important to the intellectual community, their methods of working must be better understood and encouraged. Libraries, cubicles, laboratories, even studios under college bells, will give no aid. The artist's need is for tranquility, aloofness, and routine.

(1958)

5

Employ the Composer

At no time in the history of this country has there been so much concern for the welfare of the composer. This concern represents both an increasing awareness of the value of the artist in our society, and the realization that the nineteenth-century idea of the artist starving "romantically" in his attic studio until luck sweeps him into penthouse luxury is an attractive plot for Hollywood but not a sound economic solution in the twentieth century.

I suppose that under WPA came the recognition that a starving artist is just as unemployed as is any other segment of society. Many people find it hard to give up the old idea that art is the result of suffering and neglect, and though they may not admit it, they fear any social action that will better the artist's condition. For this reason, it is heartening to see foundations, government, and organizations of all sorts, paying attention to the problem.

The romantic myth, however, still influences our actions too much, and it might be well to examine the ways in which a composer can make a living. There have been times when the artist was a wandering minstrel, living from hand-to-mouth as best he could. There also have been times when he was a valued contributor to church and court. Probably more great composers have produced well under conditions of stable employment than of want.

The composer rarely has been able to make his living by composition alone, and one wonders if he would want to. One of the major attributes of most artists is great energy. Such energy is almost as necessary as sensitivity, but it is often not used up in creative production. The composer turns, for this reason, to performing or conducting or teaching, not only because these are better paying jobs, but because they use up energy and contribute to intellectual and artistic growth.

He may even turn to business or to some other profession, composing as best he can in his free time. To run an insurance business, like Ives, or to be a naval officer, like Roussel, is not a very good way to stimulate artistic growth, even though it might free one from some of the dangers of overprofessionalism. Composers may live on subsidies of one sort or another not dependent upon the performance of set duties, but most subsidies demand not merely the writing of music but other obligations such as performing, conducting, or teaching. Something in the American temperament makes the artist feel that it is his right to be employed rather than to be supported from subsidy or independent means.

When we examine the various fields of employment open to the composer, we realize the dilemma that faces him. To be a concert performer in the United States is a profession so highly competitive and so enmeshed in the managerial system that it is almost beyond the hope of any young musician, let alone a composer. The audience, owing to the influence of recordings, demands a virtuosity that leaves little time for contact with the living stream of contemporary music, and none for writing.

Conducting also holds out little economic possibility for the American composer. Our orchestras employ foreign conductors who aspire to compose, but very few Americans. The reason for this is not just our cultural inferiority complex, but the enormous social complexity of our orchestral institutions. Even if the American composer could find adequate training as a conductor, which usually he cannot, he could not carry on the demands of the job and still develop as a composer. Conducting, therefore, is unrealistic as a steady source of income.

New fields of employment have opened up for the composer that never existed before: the communications industries, including cinema, radio, television, recording, and electronics. These jobs, however, make demands upon the composer that are antipathetic to creative work and require a technical training that is remote from music. Composing comes to take second place because of the routine of the job.

Many subsidies that support the European composer are unavailable to Americans. Income from radio and concert performances and from publication that supports young Europeans hardly exists for young Americans. Even the mature American composer would barely make enough to pay for the copying of his scores. True, the American's music is better recorded, more widely performed, and generally better received by the public than is the European's, but his return is not in cash.

Teaching, therefore, is the natural way for the American composer to make his living, just as it was in the past. Many of our finest music schools were organized by composers, and many of our finest composers teach in our universities and colleges. But even here, where he naturally belongs, his activities have been narrowed.

In the past, the composer was involved in all aspects of the curriculum, but today his teaching is usually limited to the theory and the composition of music. Even in this important part of the curriculum, often the composer is restricted because of the fear that his ideas might be radical. Indeed, there are many music departments without a composer on the faculty, at a time in our history when composers have few other sources of income.

The popular romantic image of the artist is still to be found in the academic environment and is the basis for misunderstanding. The artist is feared as a disturbing influence, and this fear is fed by the actions of the Bohemian fringe whose pretensions cover the lack of real creative gift. Certainly the artist is an individualist, but no more so than the mathematician. Like the creative person in any field, the composer has a high degree of intellectual discipline and the energy for long hours of concentrated and continuous work.

The composer is no more psychologically maladjusted than the creative person in any field; he is no more unsocial in his behavior. Like most creative people, he does not like to be regimented; he does not like to conform to the trivial routines of an organization; he is not a born mixer. Even in the matter of conformity, however, composers are about as unpredictable as other people. We all know composers who are admirable organizers and administrators as well as composers who are very articulate and who meet people easily. We know, also, composers who are quiet and timid in their contacts with other people; composers who find it difficult to express themselves verbally; composers quite incapable of heading a committee.

The qualities of a great teacher, however, are not those of an able administrator. It can be claimed that great teaching is founded on the ability to communicate one's enthusiasm for his subject, and many a quiet, introspective teacher who is creatively productive but little active on administrative committees, burns with an intense enthusiasm that is communicated to his students and that quite changes the course of their intellectual development. This enthusiasm, backed by discipline and leading to production, is the quality of the creative person that should be valued in our schools.

The contribution the composer makes to the curriculum differs from that of the historian or theorist. The historian looks to the past in order to increase knowledge of our cultural heritage. The theorist verbalizes musical practice, but as soon as practice can be verbalized, it belongs, somewhat, to the past. The composer does more than clarify musical practice; he evolves it, and this process calls more for the powers of synthesis than for a mastery of analysis. This process, Janus-like, looks both into the future and the past; it is this process that keeps art a living part of culture. We realize the need for scholars to teach young people the disciplined techniques of research and our need for theorists to train students in the skills of musical practice, but sometimes we fail to understand our need to transform music into living expression.

Such a transformation inevitably disturbs the status quo. It always has, and it always will. I once stated in a lecture my belief that the function of the composer in education was to "upset the apple-cart." That is indeed his function, and one that should be valued and not feared, for the natural direction of the status quo, as a wise administrator once said, is down.

The composer's emphasis upon the intuitive, the individual, and the spontaneous fills students and colleagues, who may feel themselves to be uncreative, with a certain amount of fear. This gets mixed up with the popular myth of the artist as unstable. It develops into an opposition to new ideas.

A common experience of the composer-teacher is to meet this fear in his students. What the student fears, of course, is not the teacher but himself. He doubts his own capacity to hear, to shape a musical phrase—indeed, to feel. All of his confidence has been based upon well-learned systems that leave no room for individuality. In becoming a defender of the cliché, he limits the breadth of his education and the quality of enthusiasm that is basic to all good learning. He is the very student who needs most the values inherent in the study of composition, for a teacher trained only in method never can take the place of one gifted with artistic imagination.

Composition is not a study that should be limited to the talented few in music any more than it is thus limited in English. When the English teacher asks students to write poems or essays or short stories, he knows how few will be professional writers. Nevertheless, something is gained that cannot be learned by reading literature or studying rhetoric. The very purpose of the study of composition is to reassert the importance of individual expression and to show that all of the systems that make up musical craft are merely means to an end. One of the most gratifying moments in teaching composition comes when the doubtful student realizes that he can trust his ear, and that many of the words he has *talked* about music have been devices for escaping the essential act of *doing.*

The composer in the university should be valued for his individual way of looking at music. He should not be thought a theorist. His approach to the teaching of literature never will duplicate the historian's systematic approach. What he will offer, whether it be in the study of counterpoint, of the music of Beethoven or Bartók, or of free composition, is a unique and individual way of looking at music. No student in any musical field deserves a degree in music without contact with that type of thinking.

The kind of composer who should be sought by our universities and colleges obviously is one who is able to communicate this unique quality. Personal qualifications are worthless without artistic qualifications. No amount of verbal gift can take the place of artistic insight. In fact, many an artist who is tongue-tied in the chatter of the outer office is most articulate when teaching his special field. One of the greatest teachers I ever had was incapable of systematic organization, yet every bypath he investigated left an indelible impression.

I dread the tendency to tame the composer into a school-broken pet. If that is the object of our doctoral degrees in composition, they should be abandoned. Conformity is not the object of art in a free society and not the object of art in our schools. As modern life becomes more complex, the areas in which individual thought and feeling can flower uninhibited become more precious. To demand that in these areas the human mind conform to a stereotype is to dry up the wells of our culture. Surely the function of our music schools is to encourage rather than discourage individuality within discipline.

The vitality of the young composers of this country is amazing, and their enthusiasm must be encouraged. The foundations and various organizations giving thought to the economic welfare of the American composer understand this. There is no reason why academic institutions should not accept a vital role in this effort.

(1961)

6

The Artist Must Rebel

Albert Camus has written that "art is the activity that exalts and denies simultaneously,"[1] and that "to create, today, is to create dangerously."[2] The artist must follow the narrow path between these two extremes, and his "style" is the answer to this challenge. It is "through style," Camus points out, that "the creative effort reconstructs the world, and always with the same slight distortion that is the mark of both art and protest."[3] He brings to our attention a fact that we forget too easily—perhaps because we want to forget it—that the artist is a rebel. Growth implies discord as well as advance, and strife is the source of all things.

When we look at the music of young composers today in terms of our society, in terms of problems of performance and our musical institutions, in terms of our efforts to integrate our music more effectively into our culture, we must remember that the real artist is a rebel and that he will demand the right to define his style in terms of the world as he sees and hears it. It does no good to ask him not to "create dangerously" for there is no other road that he can follow to real artistic achievement.

The artist need not fear that he will prostitute his art. His danger, as Thomas Wolfe points out, is that he may not produce it in the first place and if he fails in the creative process, if his style does not exist, then, of course, he is not an artist.[4]

Writing notes does not make a composer. A composer is an individual who reflects in his written music the world in which he lives and his personal reaction to that world. Talent and craft will not insure insight but will merely help him to focus his sensitivity and energy on the realities of the short span of time during which he lives as an artist.

No one environment is better for an artist than any other. The artist's life is lonely wherever he is because he must find the answers that shape his decisions within himself. For him, truth is something that he must feel, something that he must experience.

For the composer, of course, this experience must be in the world of sound, not just sound in traditional concerts or under controlled conditions, but the whole world of sound around him. He must respond to this world of sound, and it is inevitable that he should wish others to share his experience. A free-lance composer starving in an attic in a large city is no better off than a composer isolated in a "Walden" retreat or a composer involved with the weekly services in Leipzig or the routines of teaching the young in a college. He may function better if he doesn't overeat or if he is not overburdened with responsibilities, but there have been fat artists, and there have been extremely productive artists who carried an incredible work-load. It is not the environment that determines the artist's contribution, but the reaction of the artist to his environment.

One returns to Camus's concept of the artist as rebel. But against what authority does the composer rebel? The word "rebel" has pejorative implications in politics that should not carry over into the arts. The artist may or may not be a political rebel, and his political views may have no bearing on his artistic revolt.

Music by its very nature is a revolt against the inadequacy of verbal expression. When the young person decides to be a composer he is giving expression to this revolt and in a sense joining Hegel and Schopenhauer in their concept of music as pure subjectivity freed from the material, from the limits of space, and as expressing truth not communicable in any other form or in any other language.

To become conscious of this power of music is the first step in the education of the composer. When Oedipus realizes that his wife is also his mother he utters a wail that is the very essence of music in its expression of feelings that no words could convey. But this awareness of what music is comes very slowly as a composer matures.

Later the young composer comes to realize that music has a great complexity that he must master; it may be an art of pure subjectivity, but the mastery of its craft is a very objective business. The writing of music often seems at this point to have turned into a humdrum routine against which the real artist must rebel. What is the purpose, he asks, of mastering the traditional techniques of music if in doing so he must close the doors to the world of sound around him? The conflict between tradition and experience becomes acute and the young artist thrashes around trying to find his way in what often seems to him a hostile world. He becomes a rebel, an *enfant terrible,* in order to find his own unique relationship to the time in which he lives, in order to find what Camus has defined as style.

It should be obvious that the more social values change and the more fundamentally the character and patterns of life alter, the more desperate will be the artist's plight and the more rebellious his behavior. Which is the worse death, he asks: to embrace the sterility of tradition or to flounder in the morass and confusion of modern reality? If he chooses the first he may never be born as an artist; if he chooses the second he may lack the craft to give substance to his convictions.

During recent decades there has sprung up a lively debate as to whether the university is a proper environment for the education of the artist. Many administrations point with pride to beautiful buildings and beautiful auditoriums carefully planned to the last detail to encourage performances and festivals, and only the ignorant still contend that there is a richer and more vital cultural life in the core city than there is in many outlying environments. But the question must be asked whether the university has understood the needs of the young artist's development, for the artist can wither in a plush environment as easily as he can under deprivation.

The university is justified in seeing creativity embrace the whole of its activity. It must encourage the creative mathematician or physicist or historian as well as the creative artist, and it is perhaps natural that the administration should feel that the problem is essentially the same regardless of the special area. In many ways it is the same, and the university is justified in viewing its function as embracing the totality of our culture. But each area has had to convince the administration of its special needs. Since usually these needs have involved the building of laboratories or the expansion of library or the construction of class rooms, it is understandable that solutions should always be sought in the construction of plant. But for the creative artist the plant may be of secondary concern, for his development depends on finding an individual style, on living rebelliously as he develops his craft. It is not so easy for the university to shelter, or even encourage, the rebel.

The university is naturally a conservative institution, but its student body has not always been so. Most of the theologians who rebelled against religious traditions came from the universities; indeed our Puritan ancestors formed such a group that fled England in order to be free to live by ideals they had developed at Oxford and Cambridge. Emerson shaped his rebellion at Harvard, Hawthorne at Bowdoin, Veblen at Carleton.

As the university became more concerned with technology and less with philosophy, a new attitude developed which is conservative but also constantly in opposition to tradition. The physicist or chemist, the engineer or the health scientist, must be aware of the very latest discoveries in his field, and he must keep up with the literature even if it means employing an assistant to do it for him. In teaching science, tradition is less important than awareness of current research, and a healthy skepticism is encouraged on the part of the student as a matter of course. Superstitions and folkways will rarely influence the faculty of medicine even if the administration should be so bold as to recommend it.

The attitude of our faculties in the arts is quite different. There are pianists and vocalists and conductors who pride themselves on their ignorance of and opposition to contemporary music. They argue that people are interested only in the past and their attitude is often supported by the administration. They are quite willing to represent in their teaching a cultural lag, and to demand of students an attitude that is not just conservative but reactionary. They have no enthusiasm for their art as a living vehicle of human expression. There is often talk of the professional artist or the professional theater but very little talk of the creative artist or the creative theater. The scientist sees his function in the university as one of contributing to knowledge, and as a teacher he is concerned with students who will in their turn push further toward the frontiers of the unknown. The artist often views his function in the university as that of entertainer, not even entertainer on a national scale, but merely local. And he teaches his students to be entertainers, knowing full well how few ever will succeed.

The young creative artist rebels against this attitude. He realizes that art is entertainment, that it is even big business, but he knows that it is much more than that. He fails to find in the traditionalism of the university (or the conservatory, for that matter) much that is meaningful to him. He deplores the apathy of audiences, the lack of skill or enthusiasm of performers, and the ignorance of the administration as to the place of art in the institution. He feels that his time—precious time—is wasted on lectures and on routines that have long since lost their meaning. He feels himself an outsider because of his sincerity and his desperate need. He sees, as Thomas Wolfe has written, that he must find for himself the tongue to utter what he knows but cannot say. "There is no such thing as an artistic vacuum; there is no such thing as a time when the artist may work in a delightful atmosphere, free of agony that other men must know, or if the artist ever does find such a time, it is something not to be hoped for, something not to be sought for indefinitely."[5] He rebels, therefore, against the historical wisdom of the university.

In earlier times the artist could express his rebellion by moving into the frontier or by going to sea or more recently by going to Europe. There are no more frontiers and the sea has lost its glamour and Europe is expensive, so during the recent past the artist has moved to the fringes of the university, within its shadow but not quite part of it. Here he has mingled with others of his generation and sought a common understanding of his times. He has created dangerously and not always well, but from his revolt has come a force that cannot be ignored. There are very few American composers or writers who have not come from our traditional educational institutions. It could hardly be otherwise. But most of them have rebelled.

The common factor of artist as rebel must be understood before the university can succeed in its role as mentor of the arts. The creation of a "delightful atmosphere" may be nice for art as entertainment and commerce, but it represents no particular advance for the creative artist. Obviously artists need time in which to work, but so does everyone else in the university. The artist should be a literate human being, but so should the chemist and the engineer. The challenge is to form an environment that is contemporary and keyed to special professional needs.

Other disciplines have faced the same challenge and have solved it in their special ways. To be contemporary is so basic to science and technology that it dominates every aspect of creative research, and this attitude pushes into many areas, such as psychology and sociology, that once were a part of philosophy.

The scientist may be interested in the art of the Middle Ages or the Renaissance, but he will not be very interested in the science; yet that art may be as obsolete for our time as the science is. It is a part of history and therefore important to the cultural background, but it is not an adequate key to the present, and the artist, like the scientist, must live in the present.

The first step is to develop a professional attitude in artists and to demand a high level of skill from composers and performers. As Gunther Schuller once observed, there is a great need for fine performers and fine composers on the faculties of universities. Unless the faculty can be of real quality it would be better to leave the development of creative artists to a few institutions and put the emphasis honestly on the introduction of general students to the appreciation of the arts or the training of secondary school teachers. A young composer responds to a teacher who is himself a practicing composer just as a young pianist learns most from a teacher who is constantly performing.

But even if the faculty were of the very highest quality there still would remain the need for the young artist to rebel, and this need should be understood. The institution must distinguish between the talented, creative person seeking his style through rebellion, and the untalented, maladjusted student seeking escape from the demands of higher education through the affectations of rebellion. The real artist writes and writes and writes, struggling endlessly to find the answer he seeks through the process of doing. He is a person of action. The impostor talks and talks and talks, struggling endlessly to give the impression that he is productive while in fact never producing anything. The real artist learns because he is always seeking. It is with the real artist that the university must be concerned.

Our universities have not yet built a structure that is well planned for the real artist, a structure that will develop his professional needs as laboratories develop the scientist's. The artist cannot divide living and working. He cannot turn his work on at a certain hour and turn it off when the bell rings. He is extremely sensitive to distractions. The tools of his trade are very special and sometimes rather messy.

What an exciting thing it would be for a university to plan properly a building to house the artist! It would be concerned with all aspects of the young artist's life—where he lives and works, where he performs, where he experiments with new media, where he meets with teachers and students, and where he relaxes. It would be a complex expressing a way of life, a philosophy, an ideal, and would show the university's capacity to shelter the artist as it does the scientist and the scholar.

More crucial in the long run than the building in which the artist is housed is the attitude of administration and faculty towards art as a living force, the realization that art lives in the present and not in the past, that it reflects and shapes the feeling and the thought of each generation. In spite of the substantial advances that the arts have made in our universities and schools, the fine new buildings, the higher professional qualifications of faculties, the many concerts and exhibitions and theater productions, there is little understanding of art as something alive and constantly changing. Overemphasis on the past alienates the younger generation, while audiences are made up largely of the middle-aged and elderly. The result is an unhealthy environment for the education of the young artist, an environment in which his revolt is too violent to be constructive.

Rebellion, if it is to result in a style, must be constructive, not destructive. It must lead the artist to a positive conviction, not a negative one. The student artist must be concerned with the realities of his art, realities that he can experience and judge, that he can master and control because they are meaningful to him and to his vision of life. Only in this way can each new generation find its unique relationship to tradition.

(1969)

7

Making Music

My remarks concern my conviction that the study of composition is an infinitely more important field for the music student than is sometimes recognized by college administrations. The development of that thesis came about from the way that I organized compositional work at the University of Michigan.

It has to do with performance, because a composer is composing a performance. For instance, any composer who's writing for the orchestra, in working at his desk imagines the orchestra in front of him. He's thinking in terms of the orchestra. If he isn't he won't write a good orchestral piece. If he writes for the articulation of a flute as though he were writing for a double bass, it isn't going to work.

So in his imagination he has in front of him—in his mind—the orchestra, and he is producing a performance. Now, he probably will never hear the performance that he has had in his mind. Sometimes he may: wasn't it César Franck who said when he heard his Symphony that it sounded just like he thought it would? That's lovely, but I think more often composers say: "Well, it didn't sound too bad."

And conductors can be very influential. I've been fortunate to have had Eugene Ormandy conduct my works with the Philadelphia Orchestra quite often. The Second Symphony, which was the first one he did, never sounded exactly as I had imagined it. The Third Symphony for some peculiar reason sounded immediately like my music. I don't know why.

In any case, a composer composes a performance; therefore, his work *is* a performance. He may have all sorts of theories about it, but I can assure you that very few of them have anything to do with the theory courses that are taught in academia. For instance, the chances are that he isn't going to be concerned at all with the whole triadic business. It doesn't pay dividends any more, as my friend Roberto Gerhard used to say.

Now, also, the composer often conducts as he composes. In writing his music he has to make up his mind whether the conductor is going to do "ONE–two, ONE–two," or "ONE–two–three–four, ONE–two–three–four." How is he going to conduct it? What is the conductor's gesture going to be? The composer does that partly because of the way the music flows through him and comes to the page, but partly it is a technical matter. He's going to have to decide whether it is the quarter-note or the half-note that is the beat. He has to make up his mind about the metrics of his work.

Or he may decide he wants it free-wheeling; he doesn't want any meter, so he writes: *No Meter* with the sign for "no meter," and then the conductor has to give cues. The composer has to mark these cues so that the conductor gives them dramatically, because if he doesn't he is likely to get a lackadaisical response from the orchestra.

Can you imagine a composer writing a work that was to be nonmetric without feeling a strong sense of pulse? He must transmit this sense of pulse to the conductor. This reminds me of an experience I had in Florence once with the composer Luigi Dallapiccola. I played him tapes of my work and he took the score as the tape was playing and moved about the room. It was fascinating to see the experience of the music go through him as though he were a conductor.

A composer, in his training, studies both performance and conducting. I must admit that most composers won't be good scholars, although some of them will be. But they almost always will perform well on some instrument, and even perform some on the piano, so they will have broad skills.

It is probably true that they have unusual ideas now and then about music education, but they aren't totally ignorant about it. That's why composers have made some of the most distinguished administrators. One can give such examples as Grant Beglarian and Peter Mennin, both administrators, who have had training in composition.

This is excellent training for administrators because it is very broad. I'm not saying that administrators all must have that kind of training, but I do say that a curriculum in composition is not just designed to make Beethovens. Indeed, it isn't really to make Beethovens at all.

If a composer has the stuff to be a Beethoven, he'll make it himself. Nothing that you can do will help. In fact, I think if he first gets the idea that he wants to be a Beethoven when he registers in college, he doesn't have much chance. I think the chances are that that idea will have come to him when he's three, four, or five years old, or during the very valuable years from six to fourteen. The composer starts early.

The idea that a curriculum in composition will produce composers *only* is an idea we should get over. If it were true, we'd have more composers than we knew what to do with. There can't be that many composers.

It doesn't mean that because a person trained in composition goes into administration or into something else that he gives up being a composer, because any good society needs people at many different levels in the arts. Training for a composer is a broad training.

Another thing that I have learned over the years is that anybody studying composition realizes that he has to know ten times more about practical, theoretical things than anybody else. Students understand this. I don't have to emphasize it. It isn't a matter of requirements. The university may say that one has to know only certain things, or take certain courses, but that's immaterial.

The student composer knows that he has to know so much about all kinds of things that you don't have to yell at him. If he's lazy—well, we're all lazy. Laziness is a delightful virtue. But to balance it there has to be this very precise demand on oneself to achieve what one wants. Let me give you an example.

When I went to Michigan, I had never taught composition. For twenty years I was at Smith College and I never taught composition there. I taught musicology, and I taught theory. Perhaps I was fortunate that I did not have to teach composition.

Smith was a wonderful environment with fine composers. The teacher of composition was Werner Josten, and Frederick Jacobi lived in town, and Roger Sessions lived across the river. It was a very lively and exciting environment for composers, but I didn't teach composition.

When I went to Michigan I was appointed composer-in-residence, which was supposed to be a half-time appointment, and I was supposed to organize a composition department, which didn't then exist. I ended up teaching time-and-a-half.

There were several things that I decided upon. One of them was that for the composer analytical work is of the essence. He must know all of the piano sonatas of Beethoven, all of the string quartets—not just one. He must know all of the symphonies of Brahms. There is nothing that he can afford to be ignorant about.

The analytical work that was being done in the theory department at that time was insignificant. Naturally, I realized it would be impossible for me to do all this analysis myself; the student composers would have to do it themselves. So I organized evening meetings. We began at seven o'clock and ended at eleven. Nobody was required to come, and there was no credit for it.

We did complementary things. For instance, one year we might analyze the *Ludus Tonalis* of Hindemith and the *Well-Tempered Clavier* of Bach, or we might do some of the string quartets of Bartók and the late quartets of Beethoven.

In the 1950s, for example, we did *Le Marteau sans Maître* of Boulez. I don't remember what we paired that with—maybe nothing because that was industrious work in those days. I remember that Robert Ashley did that analysis. And we did Schoenberg's String Trio, which I find even now a hard nut to crack.

The thing that surprised me was that there were never any students who didn't come. Not only that, there were many musicologists who came. I think it was because the students were starved for an analytical approach to contemporary music and its relationship to the past.

That was one thing that we did. We were very fortunate to have inherited a situation, based I believe on the practice of the Eastman School of Music, of starting elementary composition at the beginning of the freshman year and going right on through the senior year with private instruction. That's expensive. It was peculiarly expensive because I insisted upon, and got, permission for a student in composition to receive private instruction in piano or another instrument as well as in composition. I must admit that it was the administrators at Michigan who made that possible. This linking of analytical work with private instruction was important to young composers.

Then I decided that composition was not a discipline just for composers. I believe very firmly in the viewpoint of the European conservatory that everybody has to take composition. I am sure you all know the difference between the European university and the European conservatory. The university in Europe is devoted entirely to scholarship in music. It is nothing like our universities. We combine the conservatory with the university in this country, a magnificent, innovative, educational experiment.

It was my feeling that there should be secondary courses in composition, courses that would be open not only to people majoring in different areas of music but also open to people in other departments of the University. This was a credit course, and it attracted people from engineering—Roger Reynolds came from engineering. That was his introduction to composition, and as you know he is now an important American composer. Warren Benson came from the percussion group into this course. Now an important composer who has contributed a great deal to the use of percussion in contemporary music, he is teaching composition at the Eastman School. Robert Ashley came from piano into this course.

Now, I considered that the course was a success if the young person from chemistry decided that there was just as much discipline demanded in writing music as there was in quantitative analysis and went back with a spark in his eye to his chemistry major. I considered that a great success.

I found that the way in which composition raised the imagination of the general student body in music was most gratifying. If now and then somebody came from outside the composition department and ended up being a composer, that was all right—if he were good! But he had to be good. One can talk about the very few people who came up through that course who are distinguished composers, but many have gone out into administrative jobs. It had a real impact on the breadth of their potential service in music.

There were two things related to this course that I think are interesting. When I went to Michigan it was the viewpoint of the administration that you got a bachelor of music degree, and my argument was: Why? Why not a bachelor of arts degree? I had gone through Carleton College, and I had taught for twenty years at Smith, and had never thought of a bachelor of music degree. I had a great deal of respect for the bachelor of arts degree.

The main argument that I made was: Suppose that somebody in mathematics has a very strong musical interest and wants to come into secondary courses in composition and then decides that he wants a degree in music? Why not a bachelor of arts degree with a very strong minor in mathematics? Then if he decides that music is going to be too hard a row to hoe, which it so often is, he can go back into mathematics because he has the requirements to go on into graduate work in mathematics.

A whole group of students benefited from that. One of them was a young man who wrote me from New Zealand. I happened to have a scholarship that I could give him—of course, it wasn't enough to bring him from New Zealand—but I offered him the scholarship and he came. He was a mathematics major. He had a good background in music and was a good musician, but his main emphasis was in mathematics. This is Barry Vercoe, who is now head of the electronic laboratory at the Massachusetts Institute of Technology, one of the most distinguished such laboratories in the country.

There were others who came from outside music. So this matter of the integration of the bachelor of arts degree with the bachelor of music degree became important in composition. I feel that it was broadening. There were many individuals who went through that curriculum who had the breadth and the imagination to move into administrative fields and foundation positions.

There was another idea that I'm afraid I would have to admit was part of my scheming, and perhaps not as idealistic, but looking back on it I think it probably was one of the most fruitful, one of the most valuable, things we did. I always had trouble getting money for scholarships to help young composers that I found very talented, but who needed help to come to the University. One of the things that I demanded for this elementary composition course was for every student to have a fifteen-minute private meeting with a teaching fellow. The teaching fellow was a talented composer who had been brought to the University to do that, and certain composers like Leslie Bassett, who now heads the composition department at Michigan, had such an appointment. Bill Albright went through that, and so on. The list is long and still continues at Michigan. So, this single course made possible bringing together a group of creative people.

It's my conviction that a young composer learns more from his peers than he does from his teacher. He goes off with his peers and argues about this, that, and the other thing, and what goes on in this peer relationship is very important. Now, that was another thing that had to be worked out, because composers are always a little timid, a little shy—or many of them are. So one of the most important things that I had to do was to have all of the composition students into my home for an evening in which they got acquainted, and then we could carry on with the seminar. With these activities there developed a very cohesive and loyal student group.

Also in the composition department we had a composer's forum which, four times a year, performed student works. We had a scholarship string quartet for which the students wrote, and they often would become very attached, the composer and the performer, so that there was a strong relationship. Even now, every now and then, one of these performers will commission a work from a student for his graduation recital, so that there remains that active participation at Michigan.

When C. F. Peters asked me to write a series of volumes that would cover what I did in this course, I wrote the first volume of *Making Music.*[1] This volume is essentially what I would have tried to accomplish at the very beginning of the course. I know the second volume is going to be "Pitch Curves," but heaven knows what the third one is going to be. At least I'm not under pressure to write them.

I think one of the things theory fails to emphasize is the fact that music is a temporal art. We all know it, but it's so obvious it never becomes a part of theory. But it is the most important thing that the composer has to confront. He has to deal with the experience of writing something that moves through time. That's why I call this first volume *The Time-Line*. As a matter of fact, the staff is nothing but a time-line, and it doesn't make any difference whether you make it in a circle or whether you make a figure S like a ribbon (as you'll find somebody did long ago in the Renaissance because it's kind of decorative).

It doesn't make any difference how you write that time-line nor is it necessary that there be five lines. There was a time when there was only one line. As a matter of fact I have an early manuscript on vellum—a book—in which the neumes are placed around a single line. I haven't the vaguest notion how to sing it, but it has a time-line. What it does is to take the spacing of words as the time-line. You can't emphasize too much the aspect of time. As I say, this is something which you assume, but you can't assume it. A composer can't assume it. He's got to be very, very conscious of time.

Then, what is it that makes the time-line interesting or significant? Obviously it has to have events in it. There have to be things that happen along it. What are the things that make events? Well, loud and soft. We don't have any courses in loud and soft. Loud and soft are terribly important, and in a way very simple, but never dealt with in theory. Yet they are among the most important things. The difference between Beethoven and Mozart is partly the difference between the way they use loud and soft. Very much of the explosive quality of Beethoven resides in just that fact.

Another thing is slow or fast. Tempo. How you move through the time-line. Is it metered? Another basic thing that never is dealt with in theory is long or short. Is it a long piece or is it a short piece?

These are the basic things that a composer has to start with if

he's going to be a composer. To think that you're starting at the
beginning with triadic harmony is absurd. Triadic harmony,
culturally, is highly sophisticated, a very sophisticated system.
Now, it's a very fascinating system—I'm not talking against theory.
The composer's got to know everything there is to know about
triadic harmony, everything there is to know about counterpoint.
I prefer it if the course doesn't turn musicological and become
eighteenth-century counterpoint, which doesn't seem to me
counterpoint at all, or sixteenth-century counterpoint. It seems to
me better if it can be Dubois counterpoint, the good old-fashioned European strenuous exercises in species counterpoint
where you put terrible limitations on yourself and see what you
can do.[2]

Certainly the composer must be interested in performance,
concerned with performance, and he must have endless theory.
But he should start at the beginning. The material should be
extremely simple to begin with, and the group of composers
should be organized as a performing group. In fact, I don't know
that I would permit anybody in the course who couldn't perform,
and I certainly would make every effort possible to get a couple
of percussionists, because percussionists often know what music
is all about. They know slow or fast, loud or soft. These are basic
and precise, and if a percussionist isn't precise, forget him. He
isn't going to get anywhere.

So, to return to *The Time-Line*. I decided that my little book
was going to be two things. It was going to be a book of pieces,
simple pieces that could be performed by the class, and it was
going to include a little bit of composition, an "Introduction to
Composition."

It also was to have its link with performance. I suggest that
when the composer has written his piece and gone to the job of
getting the parts copied (it's got to be a short piece because you
don't have very much time in the year), you organize the class
into the orchestra that's going to play it. Of course, the composer
is not going to write for somebody that isn't in the class unless
he's got a friend that he can bring in to help out.

The composer will not conduct his own piece. He'll conduct

somebody else's piece because it's important for him to gain the experience of conducting. But he shouldn't conduct his own piece. He should sit by and listen, and of course you will have the tape machine going so that in his next lesson you can go over the tape with him and you can say "Well now, you see that didn't work." So he has that check on what he's done.

I can't go through everything in this volume today, but I can show you an example of what I've done in the book with something that is very simple. One of the most fascinating twelve-tone rows is this: C D E F G A / F# G# A# B C# D#. Those are two hexachords. You can arrange the notes in any order that you wish within each hexachord. That row is fascinating because it can be fit to so much pentatonic folk music. Incidentally, it shows that the roots of twelve-tone music didn't start with Schoenberg. They go way back.

I decided to compose a piano piece, which is on page 21 of my book, and it's only to be concerned with these six notes, C D E F G A. One of the first things that you have to learn as a composer is that you state your idea immediately. You don't wait. So this piece begins at once with a motive derived from the tones of the hexachord, followed by transpositions to other levels. That is followed by selecting notes from the cluster to produce new sounds. Incidentally, the chords are all clusters, very easy for anybody to play, which is true for all the other works in this volume.

Some of the pieces are just for percussion alone. There is even a piece for voices, called "The Fat Man," which has only one line, three pitches, and a bass drum along with it, which seemed appropriate with the fat man. You can accomplish quite a lot with these limited means.

To conclude: I don't usually read criticisms, but every now and then my publisher will send me a criticism, and I glance at it quickly before I throw it away. One critic made the remark about *The Time-Line*, "Well, this wouldn't do as an introductory book in theory." Obviously not. It's a hopeless introduction to theory, but it would do as an introduction to composition.

It would be my hope that the university would pay more attention to the discipline of composition as a part of its curriculum. It would also be my hope that in university catalogs a person might be called a composer rather than a theorist, or at least a composer and theorist. It seems to me one has the right to be called what he is—a composer.

(1983)

Part II

On Music and Culture

8

Modern Chamber Music
in American Culture

I have been asked to speak on modern American chamber music, but I am unable to confine my remarks to a field which, at this moment in the history of American music, is limited. For it is my conviction that we are witnesses of a musical renaissance, and it is most difficult to discuss only a small part of that great movement. I shall attempt to put special emphasis upon chamber music, but before I can speak of chamber music in particular I am impelled to speak more generally of the spirit and vitality and tension of the music of our day, of the relation of our modern music to the general stream of American culture.

When I speak of this period as one of musical renaissance I am not doing so without reason, nor do I contend that we are at a point where we may as scholars look back with perspective upon a past movement. I use the word "renaissance" as descriptive of a culmination which is part of a movement having its being now, and which has certainly not yet run its course.

Music cannot build a new tradition with the same directness and clarity as can literature and art, for the qualities of American tradition in music are emotional, and these are of necessity less easily defined. This is a moment when the composer, and many members of his audience, are suddenly aware of the emotional

tautness and urgency of a music meaningful to us. Not intellectually, but instinctively, a vital and ever larger group of composers
responds to the aspirations of our time and faces frankly the re-
valuation of those aesthetic concepts that for twenty years have
withdrawn serious music from its social function.

A period of cultural renaissance has been defined as that moment when conservative and radical tendencies are so balanced
that there is a fluid tension between them, neither one strong
enough to dominate the other. It is a period when the past is
revitalized by the present. It is a moment when the artist feels no
fear of the classics, but finds in them a meaning that he can rethink in terms of his own age and his own society. It is a period of
positive thought, a time when the creative mind sees the great
vista of the future more clearly because of insight into the past. It
is vital in proportion to its receptivity to all sorts of influences
and to its eagerness to receive them, knowing that it can and
must digest them in light of present reality.

Such vitality is characteristic of cultural renaissance. No period
in art that succumbs to and apes the past has the vitality of a living
culture. A vital age is not a placid age, and typical of it is the bitter
criticism that is tossed from camp to camp. It is notable that most
people, speaking of music in our time, find that we are either at
the threshold of great achievement or are in the toils of deca-
dence. This conflict in criticism is the outward sign of that healthy
tension between conservative and radical that defines an age of
vitality and achievement.

There is no more interesting study of this conflict than that to
be found in the American renaissance in literature and thought
that took place during the nineteenth century. There are striking
parallels between that period in literature and ours in music. It is
not Longfellow or Irving, in spite of their use of the American
scene, who represent the vitality in literature that marks the middle of the nineteenth century, for in both authors the past is
imitated, not relived. It is the group which flowered during the
half-decade from 1850 to 1855 that reveals the characteristic
qualities of true cultural renaissance. During those years Emerson published *Representative Men*, Hawthorne *The Scarlet Letter*
and *The House of the Seven Gables*, Melville *Moby Dick* and

Pierre, Thoreau *Walden*, and Walt Whitman *Leaves of Grass*. All of these works have taken their place in the foundation of the great literary structure that belongs to America. All of them have in their turn inspired writers of following generations and have pointed the way to an American tradition in letters.

Yet, in their day, these works were either given the highest praise by the radical elements in literary thought or damned in no uncertain terms by the conservative. When they were condemned it usually was because they did not imitate the classics, and therefore, according to the conservative mind, insulted polite letters.

But these artists expressed their conviction that they must somehow do for their time and their society what European artists had done for theirs. It was the *spirit* of the classics that inspired them, not the form. They felt that in the vitality of their times they had as direct a relationship to the soil that germinated greatness as had European artists. As Van Wyck Brooks observes, "Why should not Americans enjoy an original relation to the universe? A poetry of insight and not of tradition? A religion by revelation to themselves? Did the discontented souls who flocked to Europe expect to find anything essential there which they had not found at home?"[1]

It is interesting to read contemporary criticisms of *Leaves of Grass*, to choose one of the most significant works of this period, because these criticisms show perfectly the conflicting viewpoints of the conservative, who would have the American poet imitate the English classics, and the radical, who sought in art basic truth. These criticisms which I quote from *Putnam's* for September, 1855, and from the *Boston Post* for 1860, show the attitude of the shocked conservative who was utterly unable to see in Whitman's work an honest statement:

> A curious and lawless collection of poems, . . . a compound of the New England transcendentalist and New York rowdy. A fireman or omnibus driver, who had intelligence enough to absorb the speculations of that school of thought which culminated at Boston some fifteen or eighteen years ago, and resources of expression to put them forth again in a form of his own, with sufficient self-

conceit and contempt for public taste to affront all usual propriety
of diction, might have written this gross yet elevated, this superficial yet profound, this preposterous yet somehow fascinating
book.[2]

Grass is the gift of God for the healthy sustenance of his creatures,
and its name ought not to be desecrated by being so improperly
bestowed upon these foul and rank leaves of the poison-plants of
egotism, irreverence, and of lust run rampant and holding high
revel in its shame! . . . Woe and shame for the Land of Liberty if its
literature's stream is thus to flow from the filthy fountain of licen-
tious corruption![3]

On the other hand, Thoreau, the liberal, found *Leaves of Grass*
"a great primitive poem,—an alarum or trumpet-note ringing
through the American camp."[4] Emerson, who more than any
other one man represented the liberal thought of the Transcen-
dental movement, wrote in these stirring terms:

Dear Sir,—I am not blind to the worth of the wonderful gift of
Leaves of Grass. I find it the most extraordinary piece of wit and
wisdom that America has yet contributed. I am very happy in reading it, as great power makes us happy. It meets the demand I am
always making of what seems the sterile and stingy Nature, as if
too much handiwork or too much lymph in the temperament
were making our Western wits fat and mean. I give you joy of your
free and brave thought. I have great joy in it. I find incomparable
things, said incomparably well, as they must be. I find the courage
of treatment which so delights us, and which large perception
only can inspire.

I greet you at the beginning of a great career, which yet must
have had a long foreground somewhere, for such a start. I rubbed
my eyes a little to see if this sunbeam were no illusion; but the
solid sense of the book is a sober certainty. It has the best merits,
namely, of fortifying and encouraging.[5]

In these criticisms we see the conservative guarding the un-
blemished, sacred past, and the liberal heralding the vital future.

American artists often have mistrusted the academic technique
of Europe. They have sought a technique more directly expres-

sive. Yet the characteristic American demand for exactitude and definition leads the artist to seek improvement of his craft in every way he can. It is typical of the American composer that these two conflicting ideas are to be found in his work. William Billings, the composer of the American Revolution, wrote in the preface to his first volume "I don't think myself confin'd to any Rules for Composition laid down by any that went before me, . . . I think it is best for every *Composer* to be his own *Carver*."[6] But after Billings became aware of Handel he found fault with his own natural creative methods. Eight years after the first publication he apologized in a preface: "After impartial examination, I have discovered that many of the pieces in that book were never worth my printing."[7] In this early American composer we find the conflict that has been so typical of our composers.

The nineteenth century thronged with American composers who, sensing their technical inferiority, sought in Europe to overcome this disadvantage. They were pioneers to whom our generation owes great homage, for they dared to separate themselves from the source of any greatness that could be theirs. They were the Longfellows and the Irvings of American music. Their transplantings were a little sickly in the rough soil of America, and they were never quite able when they returned to this continent to find the right food to feed upon.

It has always seemed to me a pity that there never was in music during the nineteenth century a Horatio Greenough to declare the original source of musical greatness in this country. This American sculptor did much to give direction to American art. He lived and studied in Europe for years, perfecting himself in academic technique. He had a way with phrases. He wrote: "America has always acted towards her artists like a hen that has hatched ducklings. She cannot understand why they run to the water, instead of thriving on the dung-hill, which only asks to be scratched in order to feed them. She will learn better, but not yet."[8]

When Greenough returned from Italy because of the conflicts of 1848 he brought no smug loyalty to foreign forms. He preached the need of a functional art. As Brooks notes, Greenough pointed out that "the true way to follow the Greeks was not to transplant their forms,—a kind of impotent dilettantism,—but to accept their principles and build from the needs of one's own climate and country."[9] To him "the American trotting-wagon and the Yankee farm house were actually closer to Athens than the Grecian temples that people were building for banks."[10] He recognized the functional beauty of the Yankee clipper. One may trace the influences of his thought from decade to decade down to Frank Lloyd Wright and modern architectural design.

But musicians returning from Europe at the same time could see nothing fine in the popular art. The other day I was examining George Root's operetta *The Haymakers.*[11] Think what inspiration a rural festivity might have given Thoreau or Hawthorne. Mr. Root dressed his performers in dainty frocks and composed a music-box score that sounds better suited for Marie Antoinette than for a New England farming community with its psalm singing and its old ballads.

It was the impact of popular music upon the composer that jolted him into the realization that too wide a breech was opening between him and the source of his inspiration. Our century has seen the gradual effort of the composer to find "an original relation to the universe." The contemporary composer, feeling infinitely less an inferior technique, has dared to stand by his own convictions of style. When the American composer today is told that his music is not as great as Beethoven's, he does not accept the validity of such criticism.

Is it pertinent to criticize *Moby Dick* as inferior to Shakespeare, whose spirit so inspired Melville's work? Is it not beside the point to tell the American composer that in his quartet he does not use dissonant counterpoint like Hindemith, nor dissonant harmony like Bartók, nor atmosphere like Turina? None of those styles could possibly have been his intention. The modern American composer of serious music is seeking so to blend style and technique that his expression will be as much a part of the stream of culture in America as he is himself a part of American society.

I am not an authority on the chamber music of the United States. Like most composers I have strong prejudices, and even though I have heard a great deal of modern music I can see no particular purpose in presenting my prejudices to you. Nor is there much point in my talking about music that you have not heard. Our music speaks amazingly well for itself, often under conditions that are far from ideal. The listener should seek, I believe, not to encompass the whole field of American music, but to grow to love deeply some part of it.

I recall with pleasure hearing privately performed last year in Cleveland a new Piano Quintet by Arthur Shepherd. It was a score that I believe to be typical of the musical vitality of our age. It is honest and finely scored. It is not a work to be easily classified according to the fads of our day but one to be understood in its sincerity.

Hagiographa by Frederick Jacobi is another work which one cannot classify according to the "isms" of our day. It will be criticized alike by those who demand that all modern music use a dissonance disproportionate to expression, and those who wish music to imitate the past.

Roy Harris, Quincy Porter, Walter Piston and Roger Sessions all have written important chamber music. These composers cannot be understood without a knowledge of their less publicized scores. Indeed, for Walter Piston, chamber music is the ideal outlet for his wit and his elegant sense of proportion. Many of his scores have been recorded, and there is not the slightest excuse for one interested in American music to ignore them.

Roger Sessions is perhaps a composer's composer. Certainly his music is not to be taken casually. It involves the most active thought on the part of the hearer. Two chamber works are his outstanding contribution: a Piano Sonata, and a String Quartet.[12]

Sessions once said to me that his idea of style was that it should be as all-inclusive as possible. In making this statement he touched, I believe, upon a feeling that dominates the younger composer today. There was something negative about the attitude of the twenties toward style. The young composer was made to feel that only a small fraction of his musical thought was compatible with the modern ideal. The teacher then would sometimes say to the student: "But you wouldn't walk down Main Street in a suit styled in the eighteen-nineties," implying that the composer should eliminate everything from his style but the dissonant counterpoint which was the fad of the moment.

The young composer today is taking, I believe, a much more positive attitude towards musical expression. He wishes to compose music which will represent him more completely, not only as an individual but as a part of society. This sometimes leads him to an interest in folk material, as it has Robert McBride; but more frequently it leads him to seek an individual expression which is emotionally more communicative. I refer you to the chamber music of William Schuman, David Diamond, Alvin Etler, Robert Palmer, and John Verrall. These and a host of others are seeking a positive style that can assume a more permanent place in American culture.

I do not think anyone living during the middle of the last century expressed in so many words that a literary renaissance was taking place before his eyes, although a good many people realized that their age was one of great vitality, of momentous conflicts and problems. It is difficult for a contemporary to know the position of his age in the great cycle of art. But one may feel the vitality of music in our day by the tension between the influence of the past and the need for an expression of the present. That this vitality is sweeping us to achievement I cannot doubt.

(1941)

9

The Relation of the Performer
to the American Composer

There is a forced marriage between the composer's inspiration and the performer's skill. Conditions often militate against the marriage's being a happy one. The composer's music may be uncompromising and unskillful, or the performer's musicianship may be traditional and inflexible. It is possible, however, that the difficulty is more than a personal one. The cause may be an underlying social maladjustment that spoils in an entire culture this union that is so essential to the continuance of music. For let there be no doubt about it, the creative stream in music depends upon this marriage.

Sterility results if performer and composer are separated. The composer will enter his ivory tower and create for his own satisfaction and for a few sophisticated connoisseurs. He will write "composer's" music. The performer will wear the classics thin until he faces audiences that find little glamour in serious music. In a word, the future of our musical culture depends upon composers and performers making a go of the union that is forced upon them.

One of the most common complaints voiced by the American composer is that many performers are, because of foreign origin, incapable of feeling and therefore of interpreting those characteristics of a musical score that the composer feels to be American—qualities of rhythm, accent, and tempo. This friction that still exists, certainly, between American composer and foreign performer is a good point at which to begin the study of the problem, for it is of long standing.

While pioneer society did not produce virtuosi or great composers, it did produce patterns of musical taste. These patterns, at first simple and functional, became stamped on the musical expression of the people. We don't know exactly what makes American patterns of expression different from those of other peoples, but we do know that rhythm, accent, tempo, and instrumental usage have much to do with it. Our modes of expression have gained some international acceptance through the minstrel show and jazz.

We must not jump to the conclusion, however, that our patterns of musical taste are constitutionally unalterable. Our musical culture has not grown as simply as that. With each new generation we have absorbed an influx of European musicians. The pioneer patterns of taste have survived to an amazing degree but not without continual struggle. The psalms of the Puritans, deeply rooted in the hearts of the people and forming some of the basic patterns of taste that we still possess, had to give way to the sweeter hymns of the Watts type. But the fusion of the two, with other ingredients, to be sure, has given us our white spirituals, our Civil War songs, and even our barbershop ballads.

From this process of absorbing new influences comes much of the discord that has existed in America between foreign performer and native composer. The fuguing tunes of William Billings, which delighted people all along the Atlantic seaboard in Billings's time and still delight us today, earned the ridicule of the French exile after the Revolution and of the English musician just arrived from the great Handel concerts in London.

Andrew Adgate,[1] organizer of people's choruses that loved to sing American works, was bitterly criticized in the Philadelphia newspapers of 1787 by his colleague Alexander Juhan.[2] The basis of Juhan's criticism lay in what he understood Adgate's professional qualifications to be, and he found them distinctly inferior to his own.

Serious American music of that time underwent criticism by performers who were unable to think of music outside of the Italian bel canto style. Unfortunately for music in America, by the time foreign influences have reached us their vitality usually is on the wane. Thus, Juhan championed the Italian style in America just as it was giving way in Europe to the Germanic idiom. German music dominated America during the nineteenth century but always late and always in an academic way. I am not sure but that professional musicians have been more influenced by foreign taste than have the mass of the American people, so that a gulf has widened between audiences, and performers and composers of serious music. The composer must eliminate that gulf if he is to be a part of a living culture, but so must the performer.

Not until the American composer came to believe that he had direct roots in American soil—roots watered certainly by the common European heritage of Western civilization, but roots nevertheless that provided him with a direct relation to his world—not until then did the American composer start producing a native culture in the New World. It is essential, therefore, that the performer respect the conviction of the creative artist. The performer, upon whose shoulders rests the job of presenting the composer to the public, must never fail to respect this basic need of the creative mind.

Music, unlike the other arts except theatre and dance, demands a middleman to interpret the creative idea to an audience. The composer may wish that his idea might reach people exactly as he hears it—he may regret that a different personality must intervene—but the enthusiasm of the performer, sensitive to changing musical tastes, may invigorate music, changing it perhaps from the composer's intentions, but making it speak more clearly and more convincingly.

There are times, I am sure, when the novelist and the poet have suffered from the direct approach that they must make to their audience. The lives of both Herman Melville and Walt Whitman illustrate the fortunes of writers. *Moby Dick*, that great poem of the American spirit, needed an interpreter so that the public, wallowing in the trivialities of Romanticism, could appreciate the depths of imagination and meaning that there existed.

There is an advantage for the new musical score in the fact that an interpreter can, according to his own conviction, transform the written page into sound. But the performer faces the challenge that his own recreative power be of such stature that it can succeed in the performance of music of his own time as well as in that of the past.

The spiritual need of his creative mind may lead a composer to all sorts of arbitrary expression which his imagination may associate with modern life but which has no real meaning to others. Since it is the task of the performer to know what does have meaning for others, he can, if he is sympathetic to the composer's idiom, have great effect in helping the composer to root his style into the earth in a manner truly vital. But he first must have some understanding of the composer's style.

It is my conviction that the interpretive artist never should perform a work that does not move him. I do not mean that all of the work must move him, for there may be passages for which he has little sympathy, but he must feel that in the main the music holds meaning for him. When this is true, the performer can help the composer materially in the revision that a musical work often goes through after its first performance. If real understanding exists between composer and performer, there is hope for a fruitful, critical relationship. But let the performer beware of aping the prejudices of other composers with whom he has come into contact. He must approach each new work objectively.

It should be unnecessary to state what every performer must know: that any composer of importance has given hours of thought to every phrase and every note of his music. Yet, most composers willingly rethink any passage, especially in response to the performer's problems. Performers often can suggest to the composer solutions that actually are much better because they are much easier to perform.

The composer should beware lest in his effort to write "immortal" music he succeeds only in writing uncommunicative music. The German Romantic conception of the composer as hero-philosopher does not fit the American temperament. In America, for better or worse, the composer must step out into the world, open to the same forces and the same judgments as others. He will have to prove, as he has ever had to prove in America, why his art should exist, what function it has.

In the long run he cannot be supported by the cultured few, nor will he want to be, for the challenge of life in America has always been too strong for the artist to wish to escape from it. If the composer considers his function in relation to the great audience, if he makes his music communicative, not as popular music but as serious and strong music, his importance to the performer will not have to be proved, nor will there be serious problems in their relationship.

More depends upon a good relationship between performer and composer than personal benefits or even the creation of music. Our musical culture is a composite of local groups. When these local groups are productive our whole culture reflects the fact. The vitality of the local group depends to a large extent upon its performers and composers. Without that combination the environment declines to the unimaginative, sterile, and traditional.

With enthusiastic performers playing new music, even experimental new music, a new tone is given to musical life, a new energy and a new vitality emerge. It is this development more than any other consideration that makes so necessary the solution of those problems that stand between the creative and the recreative artist.

(1944)

10

The Composer and Society
The Composer's Unique Relation to His Culture

The American composer is sometimes reproached for his failure to reflect in his music our native scene. Why, it is asked, when the painter draws the landscape and the environment that he knows best and the writer portrays people and objects that have been familiar to him from childhood, does the composer imitate forms of the past and not seek out new forms drawn from folk music or other sources that will reflect the characteristics of his own country? Why isn't he more socially conscious?

This question is not asked by the left alone. It is asked by all those who long for the maturity of American music; it is asked perhaps most frequently by the composer of his own conscience, for what stability would it not give, what gratification, if he could feel that he too reflected something of the greatness of a vigorous country. But a composer does not reflect, he projects, and he should give some thought to that fact.

There is a tendency for people to think of the arts as being similar. In reality their differences are striking and obvious, and these differences are most apparent when one examines the way in which an art associates itself with human experience. Visual association is a fundamental part of painting in spite of experiments with abstraction. Realism in literature, or the absence of it, is based on human behavior.

In music, however, association with natural sounds is a superficial element, the exceptions of a few cuckoo imitations only proving the point. Even film composers realize how unimportant and even dangerous are literalisms.

Music is different from the other arts in that the associative element is fabricated by the composer. It exists largely within the musical score. Musicians realize that to relate the "knock of fate" of Beethoven's Fifth Symphony to the hammer bird is not pertinent to an understanding of the music. What *is* pertinent is to discover the extent to which Beethoven associates all of the material of his first movement to that single motif.

Listeners may enjoy all sorts of unique and perhaps irrelevant associations with the experience of hearing music, but the universal meaning of a composition must come from the music itself, must be projected from within the music out to the listener. This fact should be remembered when we discuss the relation of music to society. We must understand the function of music not in literary or graphic, but in musical terms.

On the other hand, one easily can exaggerate the abstract quality of music. While it is true that a musical statement results from formal and tonal patterns, and the curves and juxtaposition of planned sounds, the emotional experience that results, though below the level of consciousness, is nonetheless real. Music seems abstract because the emotional experience is impossible to label. It can be discussed only in terms of music: "The music means what the notes mean."[1]

Roger Sessions, in what I think is a very brilliant paper, points out that Wagner's music in the Prelude to *Tristan und Isolde* "tells us nothing specifically about Tristan and Isolde, as concrete individuals. . . . Does it tell us, then, specifically, anything about love and tragedy which we could identify as such without the aid of the dramatic and poetic images with which Wagner so richly supplies us? It seems to me that the answer in each case is, inevitably, a negative one."[2] The Prelude stirs up, rather, through its purely formal and musical design (its long emphasis of the dominant and its final failure to resolve) the tensions and stresses that are the substructure of labeled emotion. This basic stuff of emotion is no more abstract than the labeled emotions are. We have all felt these tensions in the pit of the stomach when we have been deeply moved; our lives are a succession of such feelings. But the composer translates these feelings into musical design.

I recall standing in the streets of a bombed city shortly after its evacuation during the Second World War and realizing that music might very well be a closer and less abstract record of the way one felt on such an occasion than a painter's sketch of twisted streetcar tracks and blasted trees with fragments hanging from the stubs of branches. It would certainly be more powerful than the attempt of the journalist to describe the scene. But I realized, too, that one advantage the painter and the writer have, if it is an advantage, the composer never would have: any attempt to be literal or specific would destroy the power of music's expression, not enhance it. Perhaps the composer could move an audience and make it feel the intensities that he had felt, but as long as he limited himself to music alone, he could not give date or label to his expression.

It is clear that if we wish to inquire into the manner in which music can become a part of our culture, we must first understand the special qualities of the function of music. Music's function is to excite and in some mysterious way to put into order those basic tensions and releases that seem to accompany human emotion. Every factor of musical technique lends itself to this purpose: rhythm, tonal relationship, the sweep of melody, harmonic color, instrumental qualities. The composer may indulge himself in all sorts of dialectics, either for his own pleasure or to enhance the solidity of his style, but the basic function of music is this emotional one. This function is not nationalistic, can in no way be nationalistic, will be damaged by any attempt to give it a nationalistic veneer. The value of music to society will be in direct proportion to the success with which it carries out its expressive function.

As Horatio Greenough so aptly remarked, "In art, as in nature, the soul, the purpose of a work will never fail to be proclaimed in that work in proportion to the subordination of the parts to the whole, of the whole to the function."[3] To ignore "the subordination of the parts to the whole, of the whole to the function" may lead the critic to a false demand that can only confuse and frustrate the creative artist. It seems to me false to demand that the American composer reflect his native scene.

It is contended that a democratic society should leave the artist free to express himself as an individual, but American society has never taken this liberal viewpoint, and perhaps it never should. From the very beginning of our culture, art has been linked to social demands, and excessive individualism in the artist has been frowned upon.

The history of music in America can be studied only in terms of the relation of music to religious ceremony, to school activity, to political and social events. Not until the end of the nineteenth century did music in this country become an art in its own right, and it never has been free from the criticism of those who estimate it, not in terms of its own function, but in the traditional American terms of its usefulness. We are not inclined to argue today for excessive individualism, since too many of the ills of our society can be traced to such abuse, but we should be willing in a democratic society to encourage the artist to develop his individuality to its fullest expression as long as that expression communicates itself to others.

A chauvinistic criticism, especially with its overemphasis on folksong, harms the composer because of its negative stance. So much criticism of music during this century has been based on what the well-groomed composer does not write: diminished-seventh chords, chords of almost any variety. Criticism that has the expressive style of the composer all worked out in advance— all that you have to do is to add a touch of "Laredo" and a dash of the "lone prairie"—is too negative to be of much interest to anyone who looks upon music as a language for expressing something that no other art can express.

The music of folksong rarely rises from the folk; it is rather music inherited from the past and represents a cultural lag. I think I would be qualified to argue for the wealth of inspiration that can be found in folksong. The young composer may love and sing folksong like anyone else, but he must beware lest he confuse his own language with the language of folksong. Let him warm himself at the fire, learning something, perhaps, of how the old, transplanted melodies throw off sparks, but let him beware not to borrow the heat to take the place of a warmth his own expression lacks. If his own melody is worth the writing, he will find that it inevitably conflicts with the borrowed melodies, and the style that results, lacking unity or conviction, will not contribute to American culture. The composer may destroy his own integrity in seeking to be a part of something long vanished.

The composer should seek instead a positive aesthetics, based on a full understanding of the function of his art. He should think of his idiom—his style—as something which is all-inclusive and not based on the exclusion of any musical method. He should have the courage to pursue his craft seriously, with exhaustive thoroughness and understanding, and he should then demand that critic and public value his statement in its own terms. He must project his art into American culture, not reflect elements that someone else has labeled American.

The composer cannot accomplish this aim without understanding from the people with whom he associates. The educational institution has a particular obligation to the young creative artist. It may be the guardian of a creative talent during its most impressionable years. If university teaching is alive and dynamic, it may stimulate growth and maturity; if it is tradition-bound and negative, it will encourage the creative mind to find an escape, and that escape may not lead to real growth. The artistic environment of the university, like the scientific environment, must be alive to growth, to change, and to new ideas. When the university fails to provide such a milieu for the arts, its injury to the student-artist is significant indeed, but not as significant as its injury to itself as an institution and to the society that it is presumed to represent.

The university tends to fear the creative mind, and in so doing encourages the false assumption that the young composer must learn to separate craft from expression, that the technical and theoretical aspects of music run parallel to but separate from the creative. In the hands of a creative artist, such a separation is fictitious; in the hands of a teacher without creative insight but with an actual fear of the creative enthusiasm of a young composer, such a separation is disastrous, for the functional language of music is ignored in favor of the conventional traditions and mannerisms of pedagogy. Teaching becomes negative, musical style exclusive and confined, and the talented student, in revolt, strikes out alone on the difficult path toward self-expression without a grasp of the fundamental craft of his art.

Instead of fearing the creative mind, the university, doing all it can to encourage original thought, must lead the young artist. It must demand of him mastery of technique, breadth of knowledge, and understanding of all the ramifications of his art. It must do so without becoming pedantic or pompous. It must be able at every turn to encourage its students, and its creative teachers, to make that next step forward along the road to mastery of expression.

The university cannot accomplish this purpose unless it recognizes the differences of function between the arts, demanding of music only that which music rightly can accomplish; unless it maintains a standard of good teaching that is positive in its criticism and its understanding of creative processes; unless it provides an audience that is sympathetic to and discerning of the individual expressive intentions of the growing artist.

The university must give up the Romantic idea that genius produces great art full blown and without aid. The slow evolution of the artist must be the major concern of the pedagogy of our educational institutions. It must help the artist to achieve maturity. When we look back over two hundred years of American music, the failure of our composers has not been their lack of social consciousness. It has been their failure to mature into creative artists of real stature, their failure to project into American culture a musical equivalent of *Moby Dick*.

The training of the musician was never a simple matter. In 1653 the "stationer" wrote "to the Ingenious Reader," in his preface to *Renatus Des Cartes Excellent Compendium of Musick: with necessary and judicious Animadversions thereon By a person of Honour*, what it took to be a good musician. The breadth of knowledge demanded in this seventeenth-century translation of Descartes is appalling to us today, and we cannot suppress a smile when reading this old quotation, but the emphasis here placed on craft, on philosophy, and even on the mystery of art is still valid.

> To a Complete Musitian (please you, to understand Him to be such, as hath not only Nibbled at, but swallowed the whole Theory of Musick; . . .) is required a more then superficial insight into all kinds of Humane Learning. For, He must be a Physiologist; that He may demonstrate the Creation, Nature, Proprieties, and Effects of a Natural Sound. A Philologer, . . . An Arithmetician, . . . A Geometrician; . . . A Poet; . . . A Mechanique; . . . A Metallist; . . . An Anatomist; . . . A Melothetick; to lay down a demonstrative method for the Composing, or Setting of all Tunes, and Ayres. And, lastly, He must be so far a Magician, as to excite Wonder, with reducing into Practice the Thaumaturgical, or admirable Secrets of Musick: I meane, the Sympathies and Antipathies betwixt Consounds and Dissounds.[4]

The music department of a university perhaps can escape giving courses in Thaumaturgy, but it must resist also those forces both chauvinistic and pedagogical that would cheat its students of sound and imaginative guidance. Its young artists should not leave the ivied halls with a feeling that years have been wasted in an environment that fears living art.

(1948)

11

Music and the
Human Need

My friend, the distinguished American physicist Merle A. Tuve, said that what is needed in the world is not more emphasis on science, but a renewed emphasis on the humanities.[1] Our society is coming more and more to understand how pressing is the need for a broader cultural philosophy. Although our emphasis on material things has been perhaps an inevitable result of a pioneer society, we can hardly continue to ignore, to the extent that we do, the spiritual qualities that can give to our culture greater substance and value. In this connection I trust I will be forgiven if, as a composer, I dwell upon the relation of the composer to the humanities, a relationship which is sometimes forgotten and which seems to me very important indeed.

Let me start by mentioning two fallacies that injure the understanding of music in our society. The first I will call the fallacy of the audience and the second the fallacy of musical verbalization. They are not the only factors that militate against a vital musical culture in America, but I think they are two of the most pernicious.

The past several decades have been dominated by the idea of social consciousness. Every phase of culture has been examined as a social phenomenon, and no individual has escaped the demand that his activity be seen in the larger light of the group. When the physicist contributes to the making of a bomb that can wipe out civilization, it is obvious that science must accept social responsibilities. And so the concept of individuality gives way, quite rightly, to the concept of social responsibility. The artist is asked to filter his expression through this critical sieve of social consciousness. Critics arise who accept the social standard as the only standard of judgment.

That the composer is a part of society and that his work is contributive to social culture is so obvious that it needs no stress. But that the composer is writing for a mass audience, a social group, is a completely fallacious idea. It is harmful to the listener because it seems to excuse the individual from making an effort to understand the art of music and harmful to the composer since it builds up a basis of judgment which is not realistic from the standpoint of musical craft.

The art of music is a reality only in sound. It makes its effect through the human ear. All that the composer can do is to write music that will be heard by an individual. The audience is merely a collection of individuals, listening individually and hearing according to individual abilities. An audience is just so many people with so many ears, each person experiencing in his own way the ideas of the composer. To understand the audience in these terms is not to deny spontaneous mass response or to deny the power of music to sway people to common action; but to exaggerate mass reaction to music and to fail to realize the individuality of hearing is to distort the values of music as a part of human experience. It is this individual relationship between artist and listener that the composer seeks, and when he is told to become socially conscious he is at a loss to find a valid technique for such a purpose. Naturally, he may write a simple work which more people can readily understand—but such a work is not particularly socially conscious, it is just uncomplicated. Whether what he writes is simple or complicated, he is in any case writing music for another single person to hear.

I dwell on this point because the basis for the composer's judgment will be his own ear, and the ear is something that he has in common with others. There is no such thing as a mass ear: there are just many ears, and though they differ in their sensitivity, they do not differ basically in their physical construction. The composer knows perfectly well that sound impinging upon the consciousness of the listener will produce some sensations that all people of the same culture have in common and some sensations through association that they do not have in common and over which he cannot have the slightest control. He develops his music, therefore, giving as great an emphasis as he can to what is common in people's hearing. When he ventures, as he must, upon his own individual path as a composer, he knows that the only measurement that can exist between his own idea and the hearing of the audience is the ear. This instrument he has in common with all; this alone he can trust. As long as everything that he writes has been truly and honestly judged by his own ear, he knows that in time other ears can respond. The composer's ear is of course highly trained and highly sensitive and the music that he writes may at first sound strange to the untrained ear, but if it has been based on the judgment of the ear and not the judgment of the mind alone, then in time other ears will hear the same beauty of sound that the composer has heard. In a word, the only basis of his judgment is the knowledge that what he hears he can make another person hear, and it does not matter whether that other person is alone listening to his music or one of a great audience.

In music, more perhaps than in any other art, the process is of one creative individual speaking directly to another individual. If the individual listener allows the mental process of association to impose personal memories and reactions upon the music, he may listen, but he will not hear—just as in painting one may look but not see. As Stravinsky has said:

> Most people like music because it gives them certain emotions, such as joy, grief, sadness, an image of nature, a subject for daydreams, or—still better—oblivion from "everyday life." . . . Music would not be worth much if it were reduced to such an end. When people have learned to love music for itself, when they listen with other ears, their enjoyment will be of a far higher and more potent order, and they will be able to judge it on a higher plane and realise its intrinsic value.[2]

What are the intrinsic values of music? What is this higher and more potent order that we may hear in music if we listen with other ears? It has to do with those patterns of sound that make listening to music memorable. I often think of the musical experience as being like a flight. After the gala preparations and the ticket buying, we find ourselves in a plane with the door closed and the engines tuned. With the first movement of the plane as it pulls away from the airport, we become a part of an event which is measured by time but which is given meaning by the way in which other functions take place within time. With a slow introduction we pull out to the end of the runway. Then with terrific force and with sudden change of tempo we rush along the ground on a static level but with great momentum. Suddenly we rise, and we follow a projected arc which carries us to a point over another airfield. We do not dive headfirst into the ground. We achieve a position above the airport and we carry out a maneuver of landing, a circling, a change of tempo, and then suddenly we are once again on the ground, still moving but with the brakes gradually stopping our movement. We may talk about the sunset or the lovely cloud effects, but the basic experience of the flight has been the carrying out precisely of certain fundamental aeronautic functions in which we as passengers are actively involved though we may not be consciously aware of them.

The composer is the pilot of such a musical flight, and he too is concerned with certain functions in which the listener must actively participate until the music is

> heard so deeply
> That it is not heard at all, but you are the music
> While the music lasts.[3]

I like my analogy of the musical experience to flight, for it emphasizes the degree to which that experience exists in the present. The experience of flight is neither in the past nor in the future; it is lived in the present alone and its meanings and values must be understood in terms of the immediacy of the experience. So, too, with music: it is the art, as Stravinsky says, "in which man realises the present. By the imperfection of his nature, man is doomed to submit to the passage of time—to its categories of past and future—without ever being able to give substance, and therefore stability, to the category of the present."[4] Music's sole purpose is to establish order in this realm—to bring about this unique co-ordination between man and time. The musical score has no meaning until performance has once again given it existence in the present.

To talk about the extramusical associations that come to your mind when you listen to music—the sunsets and the cloud formations of our musical flight—is merely to escape active participation in the fundamental musical experience. Any factor of performance, prejudice, or thought that carries the mind of the listener, even momentarily, away from the thread of the sound will defeat the fullest participation in the music, for, unlike flight, one's body is not moving along with the events; it is one's mind; and the composer cannot trap the mind of the listener as the pilot can trap the body of the passenger within the plane. The composer must depend upon the volition of the listener to concentrate his whole sensory being upon the musical statement. Only by such concentration does the listener participate in the music.

Musical form and pattern result from inner functions exactly as the flight of the airplane results from the aeronautic functions that are carried out by the pilot. Very often people misunderstand these inner musical functions that bring about musical form.

The architect and the commercial designer are taught that form is the result of function plus means. This formula makes a good deal of sense. If you build a bridge and there is only rock and no wood in the area, you build a bridge that has the special form that rock gives, or if the river is particularly wide and the function demanded of the span beyond the strength of stone and wood, you may have to bring in steel, which will greatly alter the form of the bridge. To build a house that looks like a ship or a newspaper building that looks like a cathedral is to ignore the function of architecture and therefore to distort the form. Good taste in design—good styling—cannot accept such distortion. In the long run the inappropriateness of the form will distress the owner and perhaps undermine the functional usefulness of the article. The risk is a dangerous one for a designer to take.

The principle of fashion, however, often works in opposition to the idea of functional form. Fashion often encourages the unfunctional, since it demands change of appearance even though the function does not and cannot alter. Fashion may lead to form that is unrelated to function.

The architect and the designer are fortunate because they are usually quite sure of the function of the article they are designing. Nobody will debate the function of a house or of a toaster because it is perfectly obvious. The means, also, is obvious. You just don't build a toaster out of paper or a car out of rock. There is certainly a range of choice, and selection is important—particularly when it comes to cost—but there is no confusion as to what we mean by "means." This formula of the architect is clear when applied to architecture, but when it is applied to the other arts we are not always sure just what we are talking about.

What is "function" in music? Do we mean music-that-is-written-to-be-played-at-the-football-game? This is certainly one "social function" of music, but is it what we mean when we speak of function in music? When we speak of means are we referring to the band that performs the music at the game, or are we referring to the traditions of Western music that make our band sound very different from a Chinese band? What are we talking about when we say the means of music?

When my colleagues try to make social function plus performance means equal form in music they come to silly conclusions. Consider the music of the "Star-Spangled Banner." The social function—a drinking song for the Anacreon Society of eighteenth-century London; the performance means—the slightly inebriated pre-barbershop singers of that club devoted to good eating. Now these two are supposed to add up to "form." Well, what form are we talking about, the simple form of that drinking song as it was in the eighteenth century or the music as it stands now when performed by a great brass band? Or consider a work by Bach written for the intimate court of some aristocrat to be performed on the tiny clavichord. Today it may be performed on a pianoforte for an audience of six thousand, or,

indeed, for a much larger radio or television audience. Both social function and means of performance are totally different from
those that Bach had in mind. But does this modern change alter
the *form* of Bach's music? I think not, since the form has come
from less obvious internal forces. In both cases function has
been inner function, not social function, and means has had to
do not so much with the performance medium as with the vocabulary of Western music as a language.

If the architect's formula is related to the inner stuff of music
then it makes very good sense indeed and can help to clarify
what is meant by actively participating in the musical experience.
The inner functions of music plus the means of communication
do add up to musical form, a musical form which is entirely
internal. To be aware of these inner functions and at home with
the language of musical communication and as a result to feel
and to understand the pattern that makes music memorable demand careful listening and active hearing.

Our second fallacy is the fallacy of musical verbalization—
words, talk, criticism. As Stravinsky said, "What does it matter
whether [Beethoven's] Third Symphony was inspired by the figure of Buonaparte the Republican or Napoleon the Emperor? It is
only the music that matters. But to talk music is risky, and entails
responsibility. Therefore some find it preferable to seize on side-
issues. It is easy, and enables you to pass as a deep thinker."[5]

To talk music is often merely an escape from the experience of
hearing and it reveals the shallowness of the individual who
refuses to be a part of a living humanism. Both of these fallacies—the fallacy of the mass audience and the fallacy of musical
verbalization—are used as escapes by the individual who cannot
or will not be a functioning part of his own culture. Therefore,
when you consider Tuve's idea that what the world needs is
greater emphasis on the spiritual qualities of the humanities, remember that in the field of music this demands active participation as an individual. It will do little good to think about the mass
audience, since the mass audience is simply a collection of individuals. It will do harm to escape into talk about music unless
one accepts as an individual the responsibility of actively participating in the music.

What do I mean by active participation in music? I mean, of course, loving music for itself, listening to it with your ears, hearing in it those intrinsic values that belong to music and music alone. There are only two ways in which an individual can actively participate in an art: he can either produce it or he can live it as the creative artist intended him to. It is not a simple matter to compose music and there never can be as large a group of "Sunday composers" as there are "Sunday painters." But active participation in music—active hearing—doesn't demand that a person create music. Music is written by the composer for that great group of individuals for whom the art has meaning. There is, however, a wonderful mid-ground in music—the area of performance, which is halfway between the creative process and the listening process. While to perform music doesn't insure active listening on the part of the performer, it nevertheless does more than anything else to make the individual one with the music. One cannot perform music as a part of a string quartet unless one listens as an individual to the music that is produced. The person who plays chamber music or sings with a choral group has little time to talk about music. The fallacies of mass audience and musical verbalization have little effect on the person who with devotion and pleasure is producing music.

Modern science has given the arts many inventions that seem, and truly are, wonderful. We cannot exaggerate the contribution of the phonograph and the radio as mediums for bringing the art of music to people. But we must realize that they do not insure, by any means, active participation in the art. Indeed, they insure almost the opposite unless great care is taken. It is pleasant to sit by the fire and turn on your favorite record, but by doing this you may only be indulging in animal comforts and not at all joining in one of the dreams that has made man human.

In music, man has evolved a substantial world of form in the unsubstantial realm of sound. This dream of man to create a world of meanings and values from his sensuous reactions to sound is a typical attribute of humanism.

It is important to remember that music is one of the "symbol-making activities of man" and that these activities, as Lewis Mumford said, "have until now played a far larger part in human life than his technical mastery of the natural environment, through weapons and machines. Dreaming is the dynamic, forward-striving, goal-seeking complement to remembering."[6]

The arts, chief among the humanities, are concerned with the human need to dream beyond the material world and through symbols to create worlds in unreality. Without this fantasy of art—without this function of interpretation which comes from the capacity to use language—man's world would collapse. To quote Mumford further: "Almost all meaning above the animal level of response comes through abstraction and symbolic reference. . . . Without constant reference to essences, as represented by symbols, existence would become empty, meaningless, and absurd."[7]

And so when Merle Tuve says that the need of today lies in the humanities, he is not so much urging us, I feel sure, to reacquaint ourselves passively with the monuments of the past as actively to become a part of the human impulse for expression of the present.

(1951)

Minneapolis, 1922, The Finney Trio. From left: Ross Lee Finney, 'cello; Gerald Greeley, piano; Theodore M. Finney, violin. Theodore Finney became a prominent music educator and historian. Gerald Greeley was to become Theodore's brother-in-law.

Northfield, 1927. Upon graduation from Carleton College.

Northampton, 1936. During tenure on the faculty of Smith College.

European Theater, 1945. Service in the O.S.S. during World War II.

Ann Arbor, 1952. The early years as composer-in-residence at Michigan.

Ann Arbor, at home, early 1960s. Reviving an old love. With bass mandolin (guitar tuning) and folksong.

Paris, 1965. Rostrum of Composers, UNESCO headquarters.

Tuscaloosa, 1983. Lecturing at The University of Alabama as holder of the Endowed Chair in Music.

12

America Goes West

Merely to describe the variety and diversity of the American musical scene takes skill; to understand and explain it demands a knowledge and a scholarship that nobody to date has possessed. So one falls back on personal impressions and prejudices and, one hopes, insights, as substitutes. Perhaps one reveals more about oneself than the culture about which one writes.

Certainly the American composer reveals in his music the qualities of personality that mark him as an individual, and his music is therefore American, but once that is said what does it add up to? The American frontier—the American experience—generated certain qualities that still dominate attitudes: individualism and the curiosity to see if something can't be made to work; rebellion against being told what is possible and what is not and all the idealism and "bone-headedness" that can result. An awe of technical competence and craft. A love of gregarious "big talk" and the fantasy and fabrication it leads to. The idealization of "mother, home and heaven" and the devotion or sentimentality that follows. The humor found in the grotesque or the irrelevant or the improbable, especially if an incongruous visual image is created. A sense of community and a love of simple and even raucous festivity. A resistance to, but ultimate acceptance and enjoyment of, all the varied cultures and races that mix together to make the American community. A tension and an immediacy that come from the constant struggle against natural obstacles and from clashing social adjustments. A constant movement, everlastingly "going places and doing things" and usually in a westward direction. All these have been and still are a part of the American experience.

This westward facing is not well enough understood as a part of the American psychology. Perhaps the artist goes east from Milwaukee to New York or to Paris, but his brother goes west. The adolescent revolt, so natural and necessary to the American frontier, pushes the young man and the young family west today, as it has for decades, not only because of the great open spaces (though for this reason too) but also because of an instinctive sense of realignment. The Yankee clipper sailed to the Pacific and many a home on the eastern seaboard was filled with Oriental artifacts and ideas. Read Melville's novels! During the mid-nineteenth century railroads were flung over the vast and treacherous deserts and mountains with the assurance that they would open up trade between Asia and Europe.

The impact of the frontier and the reorientation westward have fundamentally altered the cultural heritage that was brought from Europe. It is this change that we feel but can hardly describe and of which Europeans have little awareness. Here is the leaven that shapes the great works of Melville and Mark Twain and Faulkner and Hemingway. It is the stuff that keeps Henry James and F. Scott Fitzgerald and T. S. Eliot from being really European and sours the American Da-daist after a bit of Parisian chicanery. Perhaps it explains also why the American painter finds the center of the world in New York or San Francisco and feels little artistic pull towards Paris.

But what is the meaning of all this for the American composer? There is, of course, a history of American music that reflects the spirit of the frontier and the westward move, but it is not concerned with great composers or great masterpieces. American jazz is far less a transplantation from Africa than it is a reflection of youthful revolt in America and a voice of racial and social adjustment. The minstrel show caught at times the flavor of change. Folksongs, both sacred and secular, lose most of their European coloration. A quaint figure like Father Anthony Heinrich reflects, at least in the titles of his music, the sense of American scene and humor.[1] (How do we know what the music reflects?) There is idealism in the music of William Billings and the ideas of Andrew Adgate that still reverberate in our experiment with mass education.[2] Even the nice efforts of Paine and MacDowell to master the European craft can't totally destroy the roots of their natural heritage. (I wish pianists would play the *Woodland Sketches* of MacDowell as he wrote them without the exaggeration of the German Romanticists.) Our history of music shows the change, but unlike our literature or art of the same period, there are no musical masterpieces.

As we look back over this century (for today we can look back and feel somewhat removed and objective) we see the same forces at work, but now we can distinguish great figures and sense the real dimension of their works. Jazz does not lose its force, but from it emerges the expression of the "blues" and the freedom of improvisation, and it blends with our sacred and secular folk music into something quite new and vital, an expression not of one race but of a people. From the minstrel show and the musical theatre emerges a literature of song and the natural and irresistible voice of Gershwin. Our love of technical mastery leads to a powerful figure like Roger Sessions who can control every note of his music and make it do what he wants it to do—it is no longer a matter of European nicety but of purpose and force, like the work of Henry James.

And gradually throughout this century has emerged the figure of Charles Ives who, perhaps more than any other composer, felt the real change that was shaping our musical culture—felt it consciously and dared to express it in musical terms. His music always tries, though sometimes fails, to find the wholeness of our musical experience and not just a contrived, artistic part. How curious that from Danbury, the first westward frontier, should come, two centuries later, a musical statement of what it was all about. It is this sense of humanity that we feel in the best of Aaron

Copland, this sense of simplicity that we sometimes catch in Virgil Thomson, and in the early Henry Cowell, this willingness to try any old thing to see if it might not work.

In looking back over this century we no longer need talk of names and ideas and doubtful generalizations. We have great music. We have Gershwin's songs from *Of Thee I Sing*, *Porgy and Bess*, and other musical shows. We have Sessions's Second Symphony and the *Idylls of Theocritus* and a lifework of symphonic and chamber music. We have Ives's *Concord* Sonata, the Fourth Symphony and all the songs. We have Copland's *Appalachian Spring* and his Piano Variations, and we have Thomson's operas. We have a folk art that is as meaningful as it has ever been in our history. We have an American heritage that we see in its own terms and not as a reflection of European tradition.

World War II conveniently marks the point at which the United States faced west as much as east. It is as though a century of mass movement across the continent finally tipped the scales so that the view of the Pacific was as much in our minds as the view of the Atlantic. The fact that Harry Partch, Lou Harrison, and John Cage, preceded by Henry Cowell, came from the west coast and that their work is touched by something that is quite foreign to European culture illustrates how the change of balance has affected our music. Much more interesting, however, is the extent to which these western influences reverberate on the national scene and are accepted by young composers as a natural part of their heritage. Not always understanding the long tradition that makes it so, not always grasping the extent to which we have moved westward in our cultural orientation, the young composer feels he has made a fresh and unique discovery.

When we think of the young American composer today we must add this westward orientation, this change of balance, to the other qualities that form our tradition—love of technical control, individualism and idealism, the folk heritage and its new adjustment to urban life—and we must also realize that a technological revolution has changed our concept of what music is. If we find a degree of confusion, an even greater diversity than we have known in the past, we should not be greatly surprised.

Certain figures stand out since the Second World War. John Cage is the theorist of one aspect of our contemporary music and Milton Babbitt the theorist of another. That they conflict is understandable, but their opposition is probably not as real as it seems. From the West Cage brought an attitude towards time and towards the whole aesthetics of the musical experience. From technology Babbitt brought precise analytical procedures coming from, but not limited to, the electronic-computer medium which also questions the traditional theory of pitch, meter and timbre. Both theories are neither European nor Oriental.

In Elliott Carter's music there is a subtle blend of the traditional perfectionist and the radical idealist. Each new work, from the Piano Sonata on, shows an individual search for a reorientation of time and pitch. So too have composers like Leon Kirchner, Andrew Imbrie, and Seymour Shifrin sought a new balance. The music of Morton Feldman, Earle Brown, or Roger Reynolds may seem more radical, but the difference is largely on the surface. They, too, reflect the new position of America in the world. Gunther Schuller's mastery of craft and concern for the flexibility found in jazz improvisation give his music an individual character not divorced from the conflicting theories of our time. While we are too close to the music being written today and too involved in all the propaganda that surrounds it to speak of masterpieces, we can hardly ignore its vitality.

It would be rash indeed to predict the events of the next twenty-five years, but there are a few generalizations that I would venture. American music is of age and it makes no more difference how it is viewed in Europe than how it is viewed in Japan. Less and less will the American seek his musical education or the acceptance of his work in Europe. Neither the traditionalism nor the nihilism of Europe will interest him. More and more he will gravitate westward, either physically or through awareness. The importance of New York as the center of the communication industry may still for some years make the eastern seaboard seem like the center of American culture, but that will pass and much more quickly than one might now believe. Mass education and culture, the most vital force in modern America, was forged by each new frontier and it is this force that will dominate our music during the next few decades. No need to say "Go West young man!" He is already there.

(1967)

Part III

On Composing

13

The Composer Speaks
The Piano Quintet

Most composers are a little embarrassed when asked to write about their own works. Their first reaction is that the music has to speak for itself and if it doesn't they have failed as creative artists. The creative process is a more or less painful experience that has to be lived through if a new work is to come into being, and once a new work has been given its life, its personality, the process itself might better be forgotten. It by no means follows that if a composer can shape a musical work he can turn around and create a literary essay giving verbal description of what he has done.

A new work is always a new experience. While a composer may use devices similar to those he has used before to bring about similar effects in his music (an organ point, for example, to give his music a sense of stability), these devices are no more repetitious than the devices of sentence structure. The musical gestures—the meanings—are always different and always develop from the musical sounds in the composer's head that started the composition in the first place.

How can one talk about musical sounds in the head? What is there to say about them? Without them one obviously can't compose music, but they don't make a composition. The musical

sound in the head that started my Piano Quintet was a piling up
of a mass of sonority. It was not a melody nor a rhythm nor even a
simple chord, but rather an increasingly tense accumulation of
sound that added new dissonances as old ones faded out. Does
that make sense? I can assure you that this sound in the head
bothered me, puzzled me, and literally tormented me until I
found what seemed to me to be its musical meaning.

You will be disappointed when I try to describe this musical
meaning. It has to do with notes, with tempos, with dynamics,
with timbre. My sound in the head was a composite of all the
notes of the chromatic scale but first one group would dominate,
and then as that group faded out another one would come to the
fore. It implied a slow tempo. It started soft and rose quickly to a
climax. I heard the tenuous sonority of strings. The composition
started as a string quartet. At first there was only a slow-moving
chord that started very softly and with double-stops grew louder.
This chord grew and finally the movement burst into a faster
tempo.

The introductory chord established an order of the twelve
chromatic notes of the scale. Out of this order emerged many
melodies. Some of these melodies were slow, some fast; some
arrived spontaneously, some only after hard work. All of these
melodies followed in some form or other the order-logic that my
sound in the head had established. These melodies seemed like
characters looking for a drama, or, to change the simile, like a
flood demanding a channel. Very rapidly I finished the first two
movements of a string quartet.

When the Stanley Quartet read these two movements, I knew
immediately that I had not found the correct realization for my
material. The four strings could not produce the volume of
sonority that I had in my mind. The musical gestures were
cramped into too short a duration. Almost immediately I realized
that I needed the sound of the piano with the strings if I were to
achieve the spaciousness of sonority and gesture that I wanted.

I rewrote these first two movements. The statements were
broadened by having the piano comment on the strings, and the
sonority was given a crest by the masses of sound that the keyboard instrument can produce. The first movement, a fantasy, was

made more moody, and the second movement, a scherzo, was made more sprightly.

At this point, it is true, I was not at all sure where I was in the work. I suspected that the two movements might well be the inner movements of a piano quintet. The scherzo wanted to be followed by a contrasting movement, and I composed a slow movement that reflected some of the mood of the fantasy but was more lyric.

Something happened that made it necessary for me to interrupt my work for a while, and when I finally returned to composing, the whole pattern of the composition had become clear. I wrote a last movement which ends the Quintet with a brilliance that I had not originally associated with the material. My sound in the head had gained its musical meaning. It had become a piano quintet in four movements: the first movement, a fantasy that combines moodiness and sudden vigor; the second movement, whimsical and light; the third movement a nocturne, lyric and darkly colored; the last movement, in sonata form, vigorous and straightforward.

(1953)

14

Analysis and the Creative Process

I

A composer's remarks about his music often are misunderstood. The layman is disturbed to find that the work of art was not the result of spontaneous combustion, and the professional musician is disturbed to find how little the composer has bothered himself with traditional methods. There are romantic assumptions about the artist that are rooted in the primitive lore of magic. While the mystery of the completed work of art does not challenge these assumptions, the living artist, on the other hand, does. There is a musical heritage to which people cling that the composer often seems, at the least, to treat with disrespect. The truth is that the composer, like everyone else, lives by a combination of reason and emotion, with a mind that has a conscious surface and a subconscious depth. He lives in a world that is none of his making, with cultural problems and technical achievements that he could not change even if he wished. It is his destiny to speak the language of music, as he must, within the time in which he lives. He must fade into anonymity to be a great composer: his music must speak so strongly for him that as a human individual he no longer exists. Without quite knowing the reason why, and perhaps rightly, the layman and the performer resent the intrusion of the living composer. The proper place for the composer is in the history book.

When I refer now to two of my compositions, one finished and the second in the process of being written, what I say can make sense only if something is revealed that the music itself does not attempt. Is there something in the process of composing that the finished work of art does not entirely show, and that no amount of scholarship can uncover? If there is, then some purpose may be served by examining the process before it has been forgotten completely. These two works, totally different in their intention, spring, nevertheless, from a common musical source. It is my plan to speak about that source, to try to show how all of the notes I have written in these two works have come from a predetermined organization.

This process of organization raises the fundamental question that music faces in our culture, a question that I have answered in one way in the works that I have composed but that could be answered in other ways. There are, therefore, two tasks, closely related, of deep concern to me during the creation of these two works, that will be only vaguely reflected in the music itself. The first has to do with the process of analysis of my ideas that leads to a musical organization, a process of analysis used in the heat of creative activity—one totally different from scholarly analysis of the completed work.

The composer of the past inherited established musical scales and forms which he accepted with little question. The composer of today often feels the need to create his own tonal and structural means, choosing those that seem best suited to the end he hopes to achieve. Having chosen these materials, his work is to that extent predetermined. His second task is to express his thought and feeling within this predetermined pattern.

The artist lives today in a world vastly different from that of a hundred years ago and almost certainly different from that of a hundred years hence. He lives in a world in transition, a world in which change is the most certain characteristic of culture. Each artist must adapt himself in his own way to this changing culture, holding only those traditions valid that actually aid his expression. Every artist, therefore, in speaking of his work, must first reveal his awareness of a changing culture, and then the manner in which he hopes to blend tradition with change; and, finally, if he wishes, his fears and hopes for the future. My discussion will follow such a threefold pattern.

II

The eminent conductor Hermann Scherchen has stated that technology, rather than talent, will determine the music of the future, and that ours is not an age of great creativity.[1] The last part of this observation is so common among performers and critics of all ages that it need not worry us. The history of music teaches us, surely, that no era has lacked its genius. I suspect that our period is no less fertile than the past. But the shocking idea that technology could be more important to the future of music than musical talent demands our attention, for it points up the fact that we are living in the most revolutionary period that Western music has known. Is it possible that the scientist and the technical engineer could be more important to the future of music than the composer or performer?

Art must always be understood in terms of a larger frame of reference, but that demand has never before foreseen the abdication of the composer and performer. The great changes that took place in the ninth century, reflecting the birth of Western European society and deeply affected by the Roman Catholic church, increased the importance of the composer and performer to the art of music. So, too, in the fifteenth century when the revival of the classic tradition so profoundly affected musical language, freeing it from verbal forms and religious ritual, the authority of the composer increased and the performer became the darling of society. With the impact of the "New Philosophy" of the seventeenth century, seeds were planted that have grown into big trees, and some people feel that the composer and performer are out on limbs about to be sawed off.

What is this change that emphasizes technology over artistry? Our faith is, I fear, the worship of scientific method. We are convinced that we can understand anything if we but take it apart. The idea of analysis dominates our culture. It has worked so well in the study of natural phenomena where it has produced such startling results that we feel sure the same process will work on anything and produce equally remarkable changes. If people fail to buy our soap, obviously we must analyze them and see what makes them resist our product. Analysis has undermined our confidence in intuitive judgment. We have carried the principles of rational investigation, first used in the study of natural science, over into the social sciences. Did we imagine that this process would have no effect upon human language? Surely it is naïve to suppose that the language of the arts could escape the effects of this cultural change.

The impact of analysis on the arts is confusing unless one distinguishes between the scholarly analysis of a finished work and the analytical process that the creative artist uses when giving order to his ideas. Strictly speaking, one cannot take something apart that has never yet been put together, so perhaps only the scholar analyzes and the creative artist forms. But the point that I wish to make is that this forming or ordering process of the artist comes to be more and more influenced by the analytical process and that it leaves less and less room for intuitive judgment.

Yet surely the intuitive cannot be ignored by the composer, no matter when he lives. There have always been two sides to music: the intellectual and the emotional; or, to state this in another way, music is both invention and expression. The Greeks understood this dualism clearly, and allowed Apollo to stand for the function of reason in music and Dionysus for that of emotion. Plato recognized in his *Republic* that there is something of madness in music, that the two forces, the intellectual and the intuitive, both were valid and essential. The Middle Ages, the Renaissance, and the "New Philosophy" of the scientific revolution did nothing to change this twofold quality of music; and still today the creative artist must work, half-seeing, half-blind, with some aspects of music as precise as mathematics and others as subjective as religion. But the artist must make a new adjustment between the two. He cannot avoid the impact of his time; intuition has to function within it.

We also must keep in mind that the creative process in music involves not just the composer alone, but the performer and the listener as well. The dualism of the musical experience affects all three—the composer, the performer, and the listener. The composer is acutely aware of the degree to which his music follows a systematic pattern, but he has no particular desire to share his knowledge, since such organization is for him a means to an end and not an end in itself. The performer must re-create each gesture that the composer has conceived, and in doing so he hardly can remain unaware of the invention that has resulted from reason; but the performer is as well concerned with other techniques that demand of him both intellectual control and intuitive flair. He, too, has no desire that the listener be aware of the mechanics of performance. No wonder, then, that the experience of the listener can be as rich as his intuitive and intellectual appreciation of music allows.

For the composer the difference between intellectual planning and intuitive judgment is that one can be systematically defined and the other cannot. If music were entirely the product of reason, its structure and syntax could be analyzed as precisely and as thoroughly as a mechanically contrived formula. Since music is not entirely the product of reason, and since even the composer cannot be sure where reason leaves off and intuition begins, the very possibility of analysis must be questioned. Who is to say that a scholar's analysis of a work of art reveals what the composer had in mind? Not even the composer could be sure. All that such analysis reveals is how the analyst thinks about the work of art. Such thought can be illuminating and contributive to one's understanding, but it is not a revelation of the creative process.

The composer does not organize his ideas in the orderly manner this kind of analysis implies, but that does not mean his organization is unsystematic. Indeed, it is perhaps even more systematic than that of the scholar, and it *is* essential to the work. It provides a counterbalance to the choice of musical material on a purely subjective, personal, and intuitive basis. As the composer analyzes and orders his musical ideas, he comes to understand the system within which he wishes to work and thereby to limit his field of choice. Perhaps only a composer can understand Stravinsky's remark that without this limitation he would go mad.[2] It is the common experience of artists that intuition can operate effectively only within predetermined limitations. In a sense, therefore, analysis may be the means that the composer uses, not to suppress, but to free his musical intuition.

Perhaps it is unnecessary to point out that a composer produces a work of art by no single process but rather by a synthesis which is something of a middle course, calling for a balance of intellectual judgments and intuitive decisions. The process is neither totally conscious nor totally unconscious. Indeed, to use the words "conscious" and "unconscious" reveals how much our verbal discussions of the arts have been influenced by methods of experimental psychology, and I suspect that the arts are destined to feel the impact of research in the behavioral sciences.

III

Scientific method has brought about another change in our approach to music. Music, like mathematics, has always been susceptible to a high degree of systematic thought, but in the past this has been concerned primarily with the logic of music as a general phenomenon and not with the unique organization of a single work. Since the seventeenth century the study of acoustics has been separated from the study of musical craft, and the scholar studies a score with no idea of finding reflected in it matters of universal proportion, but rather studies it to locate its unique artistic quality. This change from the universal to the specific is a natural result of the scientific revolution, and it could be demonstrated, I think, that throughout the last three centuries, the individual work has come to be appreciated for its uniqueness more than for its conformity to type. While it is inevitable that through study the historian should seek a chain of influence, it is equally inevitable that the composer by analyzing his ideas should seek a unique note-environment for each composition that he produces.

The idea that each musical work has a unique organization explains a great deal about the musical thought of the past two hundred years. When Haydn and Beethoven explored the new territory of tonal architecture, they sought to make each work unique. When Wagner attempted a psychological organization based on the leitmotiv, he was dealing with a problem of musical association only slightly different from Schoenberg's use of the twelve-tone row. They all reflect the same tendency that has been enormously accelerated since the seventeenth century, a tendency which is opposed to traditional artistic conventions.

Two important results have come from this impact of science upon musical language that are not without hope for the future. In the first place, both by the technical development in the production of sound and the composer's freedom from conventions, the expressive range of music has been greatly increased. There is more room for subtlety and individuality and a resulting realism in the musical statement. In the second place, the intellectual predetermination of a work of art has become more common, a predetermination that may in the end establish a new symbolism. In other words, both the invention and the expression of music have been affected. Let me first comment on the increased power of music to express human feeling.

There are the extreme scientists, of course, who argue that music has no meaning, that it should be no more than a pattern of sound. I suspect that this view results more from fear of the over-emotional stylization of the nineteenth century than it does from any real conviction. Perhaps, also, it arises from distress over a revelation of human feelings that we would like to forget. Music, painting and poetry have an annoying habit of using symbols that reveal our unconscious mind. The gestures that make up the language of music are infinitely subtle and complex, and the expansion of expressive range in music today, better than words, can draw upon and reveal the inner mind. Carl Jung, the Swiss psychologist, has spoken of this function of modern art which "though seeming to deal with aesthetic problems, . . . is really performing a work of psychological education on the public by breaking down and destroying their previous aesthetic views of what is beautiful in form and meaningful in content."[3]

The impact of science upon the meaning or content of art may be the most important effect of this revolution. Just as the impact of science upon our lives has increased, just as the contribution of the social sciences to our understanding of human beings has increased, so too, with this new analytical process, the importance of language in reflecting human experience has increased. We may fear that we have created a Frankenstein monster in nuclear weapons, or in brainwashing and motivational research, or in electronic music, but we cannot avoid seeing these techniques as a part of a great cultural revolution.

The second effect of the new analytical technique upon music has been a tendency to predetermine the work of art before its creation. The demand that music must follow a prescribed course is nothing new. For centuries the art was inseparable from verbal language and the ritual of religion, and composers became adept at writing music to established patterns. When one writes a song, one accepts the organization of poetry. The earliest musical forms accepted the patterns of conventional dances. After all, our musical scales and modes are patterns of sounds that omit musical materials used in other cultures. An electronic organization of sound need not be bound by the practices of a single culture.

But modern science predetermines music in new ways that result from technological inventions. When you play your favorite recording you are indulging in a predetermined performance. There is not a thing that you or anyone else can do to change in one detail the performance that you will hear. It is a frozen performance, and there exists an absolute and inflexible relationship between pitch, tempo, gesture, and every other aspect of the music. Now, the composer could also predetermine his composition, and by collecting it immediately upon electronic tape, fix it and entirely by-pass the performer. One can, indeed, feed a formula to a computer and by-pass the composer or at least by-pass what we have for centuries considered the composer to be. But these are extremes, and I cite them merely to show how far the revolution in music has advanced. While it is possible for a technician to assemble the sounds of a Beethoven symphony without the aid of a single performer, and to combine new sounds without the help of a composer, I suspect that the artist will continue to exist. The artist surely will not be able to escape the impact of technology, but it is possible that he, more than anyone, can express the changes in the unconscious mind that are fundamental to an understanding of our time. In the de-

struction of past formulae may lie the seeds of renewal. As Dr.
Jung has said:

> The development of modern art with its seemingly nihilistic trend
> toward disintegration must be understood as the symptom and
> symbol of a mood of world destruction and world renewal that
> has set its mark on our age. This mood makes itself felt every-
> where, politically, socially, and philosophically. We are living in
> what the Greeks called the "right time" for a metamorphosis of
> the gods—that is, of the fundamental principles and symbols. This
> peculiarity of our time, which is certainly not of our conscious
> choosing, is the expression of the unconscious man within us who
> is changing. Coming generations will have to take account of this
> momentous transformation if humanity is not to destroy itself
> through the might of its own technology and science.[4]

IV

Turning to my own music, I shall try to recall each step in the
process of composing my String Quintet. However much aware
the composer may be of the cultural changes of the world in
which he lives, he is normally more conscious of the specific
problems that he must face in composing a single work.

My own music seems to start with a sense of gesture which
must be translated into musical notes before the creative process
begins. I hesitate to stress this fact, because even that sense of
gesture, though not specific as to melody and rhythm, does involve qualities of sound and movement in my inner ear. I would
have to define a gesture as movement, up or down, within time,
conveying some expressive idea. We tend to think of gestures in
terms of our arms and hands, and usually one can express the
contour and character of a musical phrase by some bodily movement. Just as you can imagine a gesture that you might make with
your body as part of a dance, so a composer may experience a
sense of gesture as a preliminary part of a new composition.
Rarely has this sense of gesture been motivated by extramusical
experience, and never, to my knowledge, by visual experience.
John Ciardi, the poet, once told me that it took him a long time to

realize that the excitement that forced him to leave his desk and pace the floor contributed nothing to his work. The only excitement that was worth anything was that communicated by words. While I must agree that leaving my desk is usually an escape from work, sometimes, in the course of the excitement that forces me to move around in my studio, a sense of gesture is born.

The fundamental gesture for a work will lie in my mind for months and even years before I find an opportunity to give it musical shape. The musical gesture that dominates the first movement of the symphony that I am now composing came to my mind in 1952 in making a sketch for a piano quintet, which I later reshaped as the first movement of a symphony and then finally discarded. In other words, two previous attempts to translate this gesture into music failed. You will not be surprised, therefore, if I tell you that the sense of gesture that started my String Quintet came to my mind very shortly after the work was commissioned and while I was composing my *Fantasy in Two Movements* for violinist Yehudi Menuhin. It was impossible for me to postpone composing the piece for solo violin, since it was to be performed on the opening concert at the American Pavilion of the International Exposition at Brussels, and, indeed, quite unnecessary, since by long habit I store new ideas in the back of my mind until I have time to work on them. I must confess that I rarely work on two compositions at the same time; it would be like dancing two dances at the same time.

The String Quintet was to be for string quartet with an added 'cello. The gesture in my mind was a long upward sweep by the 'cello leading through the other instruments and finally complemented by a downward sweep in the first violin. I felt certain that I could give musical shape to this idea as soon as I had time to work. Unfortunately, when I finally did have time, things did not move so smoothly. I wrote many beginnings that were rather free fantasy, following the gesture that I had in my mind, but none was right. These ideas were musical enough; they could have sounded; but nothing in them made me want to work on them. They lacked a sense of orientation. They were isolated fragments and did nothing to generate an environment for a musical work.

Suddenly an epigrammatic idea emerged in my sketches.

Example 1:

This epigram consisted of four notes against an organ-point on A. The three pitches that had generated the row on which I had based the work composed for Menuhin were present, and this disturbed me. I feared that in my desperation, I was harking back to my last work rather than forward to the new one. In looking for a pitch environment that could give life to my Quintet, I developed from the epigram a row, made up of symmetrical hexachords, that opened the floodgates of my imagination.

Example 2:

The rapid growth of this idea does not indicate that it was intuitive. If we examine the makeup of this fragment, we must conclude that much could have come only from conscious thought. The tonal emphasis on A probably is intuitive, but the fact that the last section of the phrase completes a systematic twelve-tone row cannot be, though I have no memory of consciously devising this organization.

Example 3:

The second phrase is the inversion of the first and ends rather breathlessly on the leading tone of A.

Example 4:

I cannot imagine writing an exact inversion unconsciously, nor can I accept the strong tonal emphasis of A that results from ending the phrase on the leading tone as a coincidence. But even more striking is the organization of the twelve-tone row itself. This row divides naturally into halves and quarters. The half is usually referred to as a hexachord. The second hexachord is what we call a "crab-inversion" of the first—that is, it is a backwards inversion of the first six notes. However spontaneous the composing of this musical fragment may have seemed, one does not organize notes in such a precise relationship without the use of the conscious mind. One must conclude that a conscious manipulation may be very rapid indeed. Surely this example illustrates the process of synthesis so typical of artistic work.

This fragment not only added a new gesture but a whole new dimension to my thinking about the Quintet. I did not abandon my earlier gesture, but I came to see that the long and freely moving melodic sweep of the beginning would be balanced by this insistent, reiterative idea that refused to move from the tonal center of A. The great question in my mind at this moment was whether the special note order that this fragment established would dominate all of the music. If so, I would obviously have to take time off and analyze it in all of its forms and for all of its implications. Intuition could be no guide here.

Curiously enough, my next step was not analytical. I turned instead to my earliest gesture to see how this new chromatic order would affect the fantasy of my earlier sketches. What happened was very encouraging. I wrote the fifty-five measures of the introduction to the Quintet in one morning, basing the continuity entirely on the order established in the row. This much I could do from memory without detailed analytical study. The row had freed my imagination, and I was able to translate the original sense of gesture into musical notes. At this point I am likely to remark that the work is really finished—all that I have to do is to write it. Nothing could be further from the truth, since all that I have is a feeling for the work and an inkling as to the system that will dominate my choice of notes.

This initial stage has been examined in some detail, since it is quickly forgotten and is a part of the creative process that could never be guessed by the scholar who must of necessity analyze the finished composition. It is obvious that many qualities of style have been determined by these early sketches—the importance of melody and gesture in my music; the blend of tonality with systematic pitch organization; the relationship of the new work to the one just finished; and, of course, the whole sound complex and expressive intention that is inherent in my selection of notes.

Even though I had at this moment a completely clear vision of what I was going to do, I could no longer avoid the detailed analysis of my ideas. I must again point out that this process is not analysis as the taking apart of something already constructed; it is rather the systematic analysis of all the implications and possibilities of an idea. It is necessary, because all aspects of form, of continuity, of melodic association, of harmonic potentiality must derive from this single source, and the music cannot grow with freedom until every detail is understood. This analysis involves much more than making a series of charts, even more than understanding the inner relationships; it involves as well such complete identification with the material that one thinks freely and without reference to charts.

Let me return now to the twelve-tone row. I pointed out that it is divided into halves and quarters. One of the first things that my analysis revealed was that this row generates two other rows that can be organized similarly, with the second six notes the backward inversion of the first, and that each of these new rows has its own very special sound.

Example 5:

Now it is perfectly obvious that the essence of the original row can be expressed by the first six notes alone, and it seemed to me that by compressing the first six notes into its narrowest scale form I came to the basic scale meaning of the row. Composers have come to call this the "source-set" of a row.

Example 6:

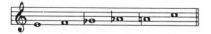

I discovered also that I could combine the source-set into another row organized exactly like the others and revealing the basic scale pattern implied in all three.

Example 7:

This type of conscious analysis took place before I felt prepared to continue the composition of the Quintet. Once I had
everything in my mind I experienced a great sense of freedom: I
felt that I had a map for every little nook and cranny that my
music could inhabit, and the territory seemed to me exciting and
ample for any form that I might wish to compose. Indeed, the
form of the Quintet evolved somewhat from this analysis. I began
to think of the work as a long lyric poem like Milton's "Lycidas,"
with related, yet contrasting sections. After an introduction there
is a first statement that uses the epigrammatic theme followed by
a more lyric episode. All the music so far uses the first row. A
second statement and a second episode use the scale-wise row.
There is a short development, and then I bring the movement to
an arbitrary close. The second movement starts with two inter-
mezzi: a nocturne and a scherzo, both based on the third row.
Then, without pause, the music turns back upon itself and returns through the statements and episodes to the introduction
which, in reverse, ends the work.

Usually I feel that a composition exhausts the musical territory
within which it lives, and that a new organization must be sought
for each work. Certainly, many compositions have been written
using the major and minor scales, and there is no reason why the
chromatic order of a row should not be used for many compositions. It all depends upon how a composer feels about the row
after he has completed a work.

I found that my interest in the row organization that I have
described continued after I finished the String Quintet, and eventually it became the source for the symphony that I am now composing. Something happened that refreshed my interest in it. I
became interested in the number proportions that I could con-
nect with the rows and that varied with each transposition. I arrived at this set of numbers in a very simple way: by counting the
half-steps between the first note of the source-set, E, and all of the

notes of the row. My first row, therefore, could be expressed by these numbers: 5, 4, 2, 1, 8, 12/11, 3, 10, 9, 7, 6.

Example 8:

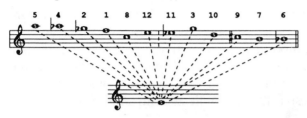

My first impulse was to try to organize the rhythm of melodies by these numbers, but I found the results unsatisfactory and a distortion of my sense of melody. When I applied these numbers to the eventfulness of harmony, or harmonic rhythm, and to the lengths of phrases, the results seemed to me musically exciting. The symphony that I am writing is dominated not only by the row organization that came into being when I composed my String Quintet, but by a related set of proportions that affects in one way or another the rhythmic continuity of the music.[5]

Example 9:

V

In the process of composing my music, I was concerned at one point with a very exhaustive analysis of my ideas, and this analysis led to the predetermination of pitch selection and, in my symphony, of durations of harmonies and lengths of phrases. To what extent is the composer justified in developing a system of note organization that then determines his musical thought? Isn't the language of music, like verbal language, inherited rather than fabricated? Doesn't all this intellectualism destroy music as an art?

In conclusion let me try to deal with these questions. They imply the natural fear that we experience in this period of transition, not concerning music alone, but concerning every facet of our lives. What has advertising done to our habits of buying? What is the effect of television on our political decisions? What happens to our enjoyment of food after reports from the medical profession? We know that we are moving toward a brave new world, but we are not sure that we want to live in that world.

But we have hopes, too. We know that we cannot escape this new world, but that it will be rewarding if somehow we can preserve our human identity. What we must seek is a new humanism. We must seek new values in art, preserving all that we can from the past without repeating platitudes that have lost their meaning. We must have the courage both to seek the new and to resist the high-pressured salesmanship that has moved from advertising into art.

I think that in the decisions I have made while writing my music I have not confused means with ends. The composition will have to live on without me; it will have to communicate its emotional and intellectual meanings by itself. The means that a composer uses in his music vanishes, while the music remains as a work of art. The special talent that is given a composer to transform sounds into music will just as surely shape the music of the future as it has the music of the past. All that technology can do is to contribute to the means. The ends require talent.

(1959)

15

Problems and Issues Facing American Music Today

When I was asked to contribute to the volume *The Orchestral Composer's Point of View*, published by the University of Oklahoma Press, I responded with something of a survey of my orchestral writing over the years.[1]

In this essay, I propose to offer an addendum to that earlier article. During the 1950s and 1960s I became increasingly aware that there was a conflict in my creative interests—a conflict that seemed to me most clearly revealed in the difference between my Second and Third symphonies which were composed so close together in 1959 and 1960. In some works I became deeply involved in precompositional ordering, while in others I gave freer reign to my intuition and lyrical instincts. Looking back on the last decade, I have come to feel that a similar conflict affected the attitudes of many composers and especially the aesthetic views of young composers. While it was only one of the problems that faced American composers, it was important because it polarized them into conflicting camps and led to further maladjustment between artist and audience. Before turning to my own personal solutions in the music that I have written during the past few years, I would like to discuss the problem more generally from the standpoint of young composers.

We speak a good deal about the young person's revolt against "goal-orientation." The problem, it seems to me, has not been so much a revolt against goal-orientation as it has been a split between the goals to be sought. In the early 1960s one group of young composers sought the goal of quick, national recognition, while another group sought the goal of complex technical accomplishment. The first group, aware of all the new devices used by the popular media for advertising goods and services, developed considerable skill in the methods of shock that brought headlines and attention to their music. They talked a lot about revolting against the "establishment," but their revolt was against only one kind of establishment. They were eager to become a part of any establishment that would publicize their work.

The second group, aware of new technological developments in the "science" of music, developed a precise theoretical language and great skill in complex organization. While they had a perfectly human desire for recognition, they sought it in the environment of the university. To them, the establishment was Madison Avenue and the gimmicks of advertising. Let us look at each goal-oriented group more closely, for each had virtues and each faults.

The group that turned to the mass media felt keenly the restrictions of overintellectualization. Our traditional institutions, in their minds, had become museums divorced from the real world of sound. Instrumental articulation, notation, theory, all had become sterile because of inherited conventions. They felt the need for a larger audience, and looked with envy at media like film, which could bring their statements to more people. Unfortunately, their revolt against musical technique opened the door to clever individuals who lacked a real musical gift, and led to a failure of the pacing and eventful contrast that command attention. In a word, their music often was boring, and no amount of propaganda could disguise that fact. The result was that their audiences dwindled, and the gap between artist and audience increased.

The second group contributed a great deal to the analytical techniques used in the study of music. They felt, quite rightly, that new electronic devices had to be used with skill and precision.

They regarded as suspect any oversimplification or lapse in logic that might be interpreted as intuitive. Complexity thus became a virtue, and they sought a type of instrumental articulation and notation that made accurate realization by human performers nearly impossible. They, too, widened the gap between composer and audience, not from lack of technique but from too much of it.

As an aside, I might point out that the job of teaching young composers during the past decade has not been easy. The first group left so much to the performer that there was little help the teacher could give except to be tolerant and to try to bring about performance. The second group seemed to be more eager to talk about music than to write it. The teacher tried to instill positive values, and if the student were really talented, he sometimes succeeded.

I suspect that the split in goals was an inevitable result of the vast increase in the means available to composers for the production of sound, and the awareness of the immediate past, through recordings, of music that previously had rarely been performed. Also, distances had shrunk. Not only was it possible to hear a tape of a new work performed just the month before in Paris, but the young composer also had a tape of *his* last piece, and arrived too quickly, perhaps, at an idea of how he wanted his music to sound. The older composer could choose his way based on what he already was, but the young composer had to find himself in the storm of new possibilities. He had somehow to adapt to the musical environment, and it was much easier to adapt if he could limit his view to one extreme or the other.

Even at the distance of a few years we realize that the really gifted composers were not as far apart as they sometimes thought. Perhaps the split in goals that I have described was felt more strongly at the University of Michigan than elsewhere, although the individuality of artists makes generalizations dangerous. I would argue that there is already a change in the attitude of the new generation of composers, but I find it difficult to say just what that change is.

The young composer seems more interested in his own culture than he was ten years ago, but his interest is somewhat

limited to figures like Charles Ives and Scott Joplin. He is interested in the expressive devices of popular music, and this interest
fires his concern with melody and the functions of pitch. Some
are involved deeply with quotation and extramusical influences,
as well as a continuity that is psychologically motivated. While
there is a strong reaction against technology, this does not necessarily lead to rejecting electronic sound-production. While the
young composer does not exhibit a renewed sense of humor, he
does enjoy composing music, and wants very much to involve
himself in performance. He seems more tolerant toward his
peers, and he certainly is easier to teach. Does this add up to a
tendency? I am not sure.

Let me speak now of my recent work. A composer in his sixties
reacted differently to the conflicts of the last decade than the
young composer did. For better or worse, he was stuck with his
own personality. The duality that I felt in my creative work ten
years ago seems to me to have moderated. I am less concerned
now with formal preconception, and more concerned with the
role of memory. Perhaps I can illustrate my point by speaking
specifically of orchestral works that I have written since 1966.

Symphony Concertante (1967) was written on commission for
the Kansas City Philharmonic and was, by request, designed to
feature certain outstanding performers in the orchestra. My Second Concerto for Piano and Orchestra (1968) also is concerned
with the soloistic problem. The organization of both works is
more like that of my Third Symphony than of my Second.

With *Summer in Valley City* (1969) for large concert band,
there comes a change. The motivation for this work is memory,
and even though continuity is still based on a symmetrical hexachord, as all my music has been for the past fifteen years, the
transpositions and overlappings I employ would make analysis
difficult. There are many quotations, in this work, of tunes I knew
as a child, but they are always made to conform to the hexachord,
with curious results in harmonization.

Both *Landscapes Remembered* for chamber orchestra (1971),
and *Spaces* (1971), which was commissioned by the Fargo-Moor-
head Symphony Orchestra, are rooted in memory. The three
movements of the latter work reveal my childhood memory of

space: Closed ("The Valley"), Open ("The Prairie"), and Outer ("The Sky"). In all of these works, literal references—bird songs, wind, and the like—appear, as well as musical quotations. These works are not, however, essentially picturesque, but reflect my interest in memory.

With my Fourth Symphony (1972), composed on commission for the Baltimore Symphony Orchestra, a tendency felt in the earlier works comes to the fore. The juxtaposition of unmetered sections with metered gives energy and vitality to meter. I have come to feel that meter represents energy. At the same time, I have tried to sweep melody across unmetered areas. Melody has always been important in my work, and that has led me to avoid too much division in the strings, a sound I like much less than unison strings.

In conclusion, my recent work seems to me much more an expression of personal prejudice and taste than a reflection of current trends. I have always been something of a maverick, and not less so as the years go by.

(1972)

16

The Diversity of Inculturation

One gets the impression sometimes that the folk heritage of all American composers is the same, that there is little difference between a childhood spent in North Dakota or Brooklyn or Texas. The diversity of American culture, especially of youthful inculturation, is supposed to have been eliminated by television. There can be no doubt that the media have changed our society, that we are more visually oriented, but I am not convinced that there has been so great a reduction of diversity as we are led to believe.

The critical view that a composer who has been little influenced by popular music is for that reason uninfluenced by *any* folk expression ignores the diversity of our culture.

In 1927 when I was twenty and had just graduated from college, I had the opportunity to work my way to Europe by playing in a jazz orchestra for dances on board a ship that was making a Mediterranean tour. Some ten students from different colleges formed this jazz band. We played the popular music of that time—songs like "Hallelujah"—using arrangements that we had collected. Our other job was to be helpful and pleasant to the elderly tourists on the ship. While the ship's orchestra played more sedate dance music in the saloon, we attracted the younger tourists on deck.

I developed two convictions from this experience. The first was that even though the members of the band came from very different environments, we all had a feeling for a strict musical beat. The second was a realization that our popular music was an expression of adolescent revolt.

When the ship got to Malaga in Spain and the tourists had left for an inland trip, the local casino invited our band to be their guests and play for some of the dances. Our tempos and the even-driving beat made the young people wild with excitement. When the local orchestra played American jazz the tempos were too slow and the beat was never even. We came to recognize the way a Spanish or French band sounded when it played jazz.

I have always had difficulty with performers who want to use a French or a German rubato when they play my music. I tell them, jokingly of course (and not always with success) that I want a "North Dakota" rubato. I can recall Aaron Copland's telling a conductor that he didn't want a French ritard; he wanted a Copland ritard. Roy Harris once explained what American music was like, by stretching a rope absolutely taut between his two hands.[1] I think they were both commenting on the tight, inflexible beat that American composers find in their popular music.

Whether the driving beat in our popular music is a symptom of freedom and liberation could be argued, but it does tend to take our music out of the cruise ship saloon and make it an expression of youth. Our sense of beat adds energy and makes measure less important, expressing a different relationship with and feeling for time.

I didn't return to the United States with the band, but went to Paris and studied with Nadia Boulanger. She put me through the paces of a rigorous musical training, but she was never successful in making me feel at home with French musical inflections. With Gershwin and Copland around, it was a lost cause. I can recall riding with Copland to visit Chartres and his talking all the time about being an American composer. Somehow the wonderful thing about Paris in the twenties was that I felt closer to my American roots.

The formative years of my childhood had been spent in Valley City, North Dakota, a small town some fifty miles west of Fargo. I

studied the 'cello and the piano and played in every musical
event that occurred and also in our family orchestra where my
mother played piano, my brother Theodore, the violin, and my
brother Nathaniel, the cornet. The music we played was the usual
trivia that you might expect. As far as I know no jazz "combos"
existed in our neighborhood.

My father discovered and invited to our home an orphan boy
named Hans Lee who lived at the Salvation Army and played on
the piano at the local ten cent store the hits that were sold at the
sheet music counter. He was my first introduction to the kind of
popular music that was produced commercially. Hans couldn't
read music, but give him the melody and he could play it immediately on the piano. He had never studied the piano. A few years
later he was playing at the "flicks." He didn't bother to look at the
score that was sent with the picture. He looked at the picture and
improvised a medley of popular tunes at the piano.

We all thought he was wonderful and admired the abrupt
changes he made to fit the moods of the picture. He always kept
the beat steady, and when he changed, it was immediate. There
were no ritards or accellerandos (except in railroad and chase
scenes), and sentimental rubatos were out.

We had no barn dances, but I remember one time when we
drove out to a farm to hear a band that practiced in a barn. They
didn't give concerts or play for dances but got together now and
then for what one might call a "jam session." Except for the musical saw, it was a percussion group and they had built all of their
instruments—tubs, tin pans, wood blocks, metal springs, and the
like—and played them in unusual ways, sometimes making vocal
sounds. I remember that they too kept a steady beat and an inflexible tempo, and this was the first time, I believe, that I heard a
"break" with one of the performers showing off his skill.

Another strong influence came when the circus arrived in
town. It brought a kind of music that was completely foreign to
our environment, and we always looked forward to the event,
going down to the station in the early morning to see the wagons
and the animals unloaded for the parade. On top of the wagon-
cage carrying the lions there was always a New Orleans jazz
band. They played a music that seemed to me almost all "breaks"

and with a steady beat that was irresistible. We would follow the parade until it finally disappeared into the big tent which we couldn't enter without a ticket.

We also sang folksongs of one sort or another: Sunday school hymns like "Jesus wants me for a sunbeam," war songs like "There's a long, long trail a-winding," songs that came with Lydia Pinkham pills, barbershop ballads like "She's only a bird in a gilded cage," and all sorts of songs we heard others sing. We sang them when we were hiking on the prairie or skating on the river or sitting around a campfire, and usually with no accompaniment at all until later, when I got a guitar.

Obviously the regular beat of popular dance music is not characteristic of folksongs. Here the meter can be very free and follows the words, especially when you sing with the guitar. I have always been puzzled as to what makes these songs American. Many are not, but are Irish or Elizabethan-English. But now and then one finds a song that reflects the loneliness of the mountains or prairies. Such a song is the version I so love of "Bury me not on the lone prairie." I have come to feel that the melodic leap of an octave is the special quality that makes this song American. There is often a frontier humor, sometimes, unfortunately, at the expense of racial characteristics or because of a distortion of language.

Much later when I began to feel that my music was unmistakably mine, those two qualities I had enjoyed as a child in popular and folk music—the energy of a regular beat and the sweep of long, singing melody—became a part of my personal style.

In the mid-thirties at Smith College I was one of a group of professors who organized an interdepartmental major in American Studies. For several years I taught a course entitled Music in America. At that time I found a guitar and relearned the songs I had sung as a child, adding a few more such as the Pilgrim Psalms in the Ainsworth Psalter.

Several of the compositions I wrote at this time—my Third String Quartet and a short orchestral work called *Barbershop Ballad* in which I literally quoted folk melodies—substituted, unsatisfactorily, folk material for real musical ideas.

Service in the Office of Strategic Services during the Second

World War brought this dilemma more clearly to the fore. I had sensed the problem earlier when I had studied with Alban Berg. He was very interested in folk music, and literal musical quotation had, somehow, to be incorporated into his chromatic musical language. In 1944 while I was waiting in Cambridge, England, to move into France, I spent many hours talking with Roberto Gerhard, and here again I met a great musical mind who was coping with the same dilemma.

The conflict between musical substance and the quotation of folk music was not made easier for me by the disillusionment with nationalism-gone-mad that one found in Europe. When I returned from military service, I felt compelled to re-examine the whole matter of being an American composer. For a time I felt that memory (all that rich heritage from my childhood) had to be forgotten. It was impossible, however, to put aside intellectually the energy drive of a strong beat—the whole concept of time that was basic to my feelings about music.

All this re-examination was tied up with other musical concerns such as serialization and electronic production of sound, both of which affect the way a composer works. In the fifties I began composing twelve-tone music based not so much on the theories of Schoenberg as on the ideas I had gotten from Berg, Gerhard, and more recently from Luigi Dallapiccola. I felt that using a row divided into two symmetrical hexachords made possible a more flexible choice, and when the hexachord was based on the circle of fifths, a pitch organization existed that was compatible with folk melodies of my youth.

My conviction that popular music was an expression of adolescent revolt (folksong much less so) supported my belief in the diversity of American culture. Each generation had its own memories of a relatively short adolescent period of revolt, which meant that diversity was not only geographical but also generational. The commercialization of popular music, though very different in the fifties from what it was in the 'teens, changed nothing, though it sometimes affected critical judgment.

The experience of composing my *Divertissement* in Paris in 1965 made me suddenly realize the obvious: that memory was not limited to past music alone. How could one—or why should one—exclude memory from the process of composing? My memory of being a student in Paris in the twenties involved very complex feelings that were reflected in *Divertissement,* not by quoted melodies but by the very fabric of the music. To quote a tune or to imitate a musical mannerism doesn't necessarily involve memory at all. Unless it does, however, it may detract from rather than add to the musical statement.

Memory is the device of making the past become the present, and since a composer can work only in the present, memory can greatly enrich his music. But every composer's background is different and therefore his memory is different. This is the diversity that enriches a culture, and it is this diversity in America that adds so much to our music.

(1987)

17

Composing Music for Dance

The combination of music with dance probably is the oldest human artistic expression. At first, surely, dance patterns were created from the natural gestures of the human body, and the musical sounds made by the natural sounds of hands, feet and voice. From the very beginning, however, dance movement was different from sound production, and the two arts were, to a degree, separate.

In time the differences between these arts increased as human beings discovered ways of producing sounds from instruments rather than from human gestures alone. Instruments produced pitches and different timbres and more precise rhythms. Little by little the gestures of music came to resemble human gestures. Dance also changed. Human gestures took on symbolic meaning and often were related to religious ceremony or to myth.

This background must be kept in mind when discussing the composition of music for modern dance. Both music and dance are temporal arts, and each in its own way is concerned with giving spatial dimensions to a temporal design. The same is true of ballet, but ballet differs from modern dance in that stylized physical gestures often are substituted for natural ones. Human beings don't walk on the tips of their toes.

Both composers and choreographers face special problems when they combine to produce a theatrical production. If the choreographer decides to create a dance to the first movement of a symphony, which was composed with no idea of dance in mind, he is forced to find a way of fitting dance gestures to the gestures of the music. Ideally, the dance should have its own form and its own temporal design. To imitate musical gestures literally can be humorous and trivial, destroying the musical statement without adding a significant dance statement.

Erick Hawkins came to see me in my Greenwich Village apartment in 1980, eager to set to dance my *Concerto for Strings*, which he had just heard performed. That work demands a minimum of nineteen string players and could not be adapted to the orchestra that performs with the Erick Hawkins Dance Company. I pointed this out to Hawkins, and suggested composing a chamber concerto for the seven instruments of his orchestra.[1]

This score, when finished, like the *Concerto for Strings*, proved to be somewhat neobaroque, with a temporal design of gestures related to the purely abstract qualities of the music. I had no theatrical plan in mind, and no idea what Hawkins would do with the music.

As it turned out, Hawkins showed real genius in his handling of the score. His dance starts and ends without music. Two Sioux Indian clowns (Heyoka) with rattles on their feet dance a comic introduction to the ceremony that follows. It ends, after the music stops, with silence and a leaping figure. Hawkins emphasizes the lyric quality of the music.

Nevertheless, this method of writing music for modern dance is satisfactory neither for the composer nor the choreographer. The next time Hawkins came to see me, he had a definite idea of what the dance would be and a time-plan for its twelve episodes. He called it *The Joshua Tree*, a morality play based on the old story in which three outlaws kill off each other so that in the end, nobody gets the pot of gold. His scenario contained humor and symbolism, and demanded that the dancers speak a few words now and then. The score I wrote followed Hawkins's time-plan carefully, but since it was not detailed, the musical gestures could be abstract.

When Hawkins next came to see me in 1986, he came well prepared. The imaginativeness of his idea snared me. He wanted to make a dance of Melville's *Moby Dick*, focusing on Ahab, and using the author's words. First he produced a copy of the novel with interesting woodcuts. He wasn't so much concerned with the tale itself as with Ahab's obsession with revenge against the white whale. Everything depended upon solving the problem of Ahab's wooden leg.

I knew how much Hawkins had been influenced by the Japanese Noh drama and by symbolism and myth, and the project seemed like an ideal one for him, both as choreographer and dancer. Then he mentioned that he happened to have with him the first few pages of his synopsis. The first section he called "Ahab's Leg." The curtain was to rise on silence, revealing the scene. Hawkins took out a piece of paper and sketched the scene. Ishmael speaks the first line from Melville's book—a first line so potent with symbolic and biblical meaning: "Call me Ishmael." This is followed by fifteen seconds of music. Then Ishmael says "This is the Pequod, Bound round the world." Another fifteen seconds of music. "Cape Horn and the Pacific!" Eight seconds of music. "Clap eye on Captain Ahab, young man, And thou wilt find that he has only one leg." Then thirty seconds of music to which "Ahab first moves. Dance of just walking. 3 harpooners and Starbuck enter SEC #25, so into (Ishmael speaks) 'A grand, ungodly, god-like man!'" Music for twenty-five seconds.

Here was a choreographic sketch that provided a clear idea of the dance and of what kind of music was needed, but did not impose physical gestures on the music. It seemed to me a most challenging project. It would be my job to give musical shape to the temporal form and, through melody, lyricism to the gestures.

It is not my purpose here to discuss the music that I wrote for *Heyoka, The Joshua Tree,* or *Ahab,* but rather the problems that anyone faces who composes music for modern dance. As in writing music for radio or television or cinema, the musical style of the composer does not matter. What happens is that the composer imposes upon the dance the way in which music deals with measured time.

I suggested at the beginning that over the years music has devised its own ways of dealing with time and space, and that its reflection of human emotions and gestures is a semblance. The discovery by Western musicians of measured time has been discussed by the physicist Geza Szamosi in his interesting article "The Origin of Time: How Medieval Musicians Invented the Fourth Dimension," in *The Sciences* for September-October, 1986.

> In the development of polyphony, all the durations of the melodic composition . . . were allowed to vary in relation to one another in a highly defined and disciplined manner. This occurred during the late twelfth century, at a school of music associated with the Cathedral of Notre Dame, in Paris. . . . It was at Notre Dame that the first polyphonic works for three and four simultaneous voices were written. . . . Centuries later, the baroque masters of the organ . . . would improvise polyphonic pieces during concert performances. And today, jazz musicians improvise several simultaneous melodies and rhythms without so much as skipping a beat. . . . By the sixteenth century, this new perception of time had become thoroughly common, if not yet clearly articulated. And when Galileo, on the strength of his free-fall experiments, distilled this intuition into a succinct mathematical concept, no one, not even he, found the idea surprising. A musical revolution had run its course; a revolution in human thought was just beginning.[2]

It is not the style of a composer that is important to the dance but the temporal dimension he adds to the production. Nevertheless, the degree to which he is aware of the choreographer's design affects the way he composes his music. If he composes an abstract musical design, his control of time and space will be very different, and can, I think, present problems for the dancer.

These problems are exaggerated if the composer produces an electronic score for a dance, not because of the musical style, but because first, the score is fixed and unchangeable, and second, it depends on a different, or at least as yet not well-defined, awareness of time and space. The situation is the reverse of the old music-dance relationship, and the electronic tape tends to imitate the dance, leading to a humorous or trivial result.

Erick Hawkins refuses to dance to recorded music, because he feels that a fixed performance inhibits creativity. As far as I know, he has never considered dancing to an electronic tape produced specifically for a dance. It would be interesting to see what he would do in such a situation. At the least, it would be essential that the production result from close collaboration between composer and choreographer.

(1987)

18

A Composer's Perception of Time

As a child I was more aware of space than of time. My life was concerned with the sounds I heard around me and the classical musical traditions of my family. I had no understanding of the subtleties of musical form, and like all children, was conscious of space only in terms of the environment in which I lived and of time only in terms of the family routine. I felt no urge to be unique. My first awareness of the importance of time in performing and composing music came from improvisation and from the experience of playing in a jazz orchestra. I realized then the difference between clock time and metered time. I would stamp my right foot to give the beat that was kept inflexibly throughout the piece. In singing folksongs with guitar I came to understand the possibility of a flexible meter, so different from the strict meter of jazz. Only later did I realize what a big step in my inculturation that represented.

As I grew older, I became aware of the subtle musical difference between clock time and agogic or psychological time. I realized that an hour could seem like an eternity or be over in a flash, but I had not yet understood the complexities of temporal organization in music.

My individuality as a composer developed very slowly and was the result of so many influences that it would be hopeless to enumerate them. My teachers, Donald Ferguson, Nadia Boulanger, Alban Berg, and Roger Sessions all contributed. Performing, conducting, teaching, all affected the way I thought about music.

Music is a temporal art. A composer lives his life dealing with the problems of time and space. These problems not only affect the way he hears music and the creative imagination that leads him to write down what he hears in his mind, but the problems change as he grows older and more mature and more aware of the demands of the performers and audiences for whom he writes.

A composition has a duration that can be measured by a clock. It can be ten minutes long or thirty minutes long. But that clock time is subdivided into temporal spaces determined, not in seconds, but by beats, the speed of which can be measured by a metronome. This is measured or metric time. Agogic or psychological time is the experience that we have as we listen to the melodic and rhythmic events that take place within these metric spaces. Our experience consists of this subtle combination of different kinds of time made into spaces. Architecture is almost the opposite; it is a spatial art that assumes temporal qualities as we walk around it.

Like any human being, I have always been aware of time as it affected my daily life. That awareness, in childhood, was largely of cyclic time—winter experiences as opposed to summer, day as opposed to night. These temporal experiences were always associated with space: the North Dakota prairie, the river, my home. Clock time was not important during my childhood. I was never bored, even during my adolescence, perhaps because of my very early musical activities. I never had time on my hands.

Lewis Mumford reminds us that "work and play have the same common trunk" and that "in these realms man gains a fuller insight into his surroundings, his community, and himself."[1] Both work and play take time and are usually done in a specific place. They both demand a set routine, and our ability to adjust to this routine is a crucial aspect of our maturity. In retirement we seek a new environment in which to work or play, but matters of time and space remain important to us.

When I watch a football game, I am impressed with how, like a piece of music, it is concerned with clock time, each quarter measured by minutes, and a field, divided into spaces measured in yards. As we watch the game, the level of our experience is determined by how clearly we understand what takes place on the field. As a child I was not always aware of this design, and even now, in my ignorance, I am not fully aware of the subtlety of each play that so excites many of my friends.

Teaching is work for me. A seminar meeting is measured in clock time, though sometimes an hour seems like a minute. I meet my class in an assigned room which contains devices for playing records or tapes and a blackboard on which is drawn the musical staff. We have a set routine, just like that in a game. I don't know whether composing music is play or work.

Even in early maturity, there was never enough time. Those crowded years, with marriage, children, making a living during the Depression, professional recognition, were shattered by the interruption of war and service in the Office of Strategic Services. After the war, time took on a new meaning for me, both personally and professionally. The tempo of clock time continued at a breathless pace leading eventually to the medical need to treat hypertension. The fact that tension could result from the way in which one reacted to time was not a new idea, but doctors began to take more seriously the need to treat this problem before it became serious. Time was certainly not the only factor that contributed to the problem. There were many social and political events that made teaching a hazardous and ungratifying way to make a living during my middle years.

The increasing impact of electronic technology on all aspects of the composer's professional life brought to the surface a concern for the time/space aspects of the art that previously had existed intuitively. Every composer in the 1950s had to face, in his own way, the artistic revolution spurred by electronic technology. Recorded performances made possible a library of music that altered awareness of the past, not only for composers, but also for performers and audiences. Radio and television, combined with recording, changed the public image both of performer and composer. This revolution challenged one's courage while growing old. In middle age, I had to find a new relationship to the temporal design—to time and space—both in my life and in my profession. I felt that the whole tradition of Western music was in jeopardy and with it, my integrity as an artist.

Electronic music was first produced, using either natural or electronically generated sound, by running magnetic tape at a set speed per inch across a recording head. Chronomic time not only controlled the recording process, but repeated performances were identical. Here was frozen music, lacking not only the metered time that had dominated Western music for seven centuries, but lacking also those musical signs and functions that imparted a psychological dimension to time.

The physicist Geza Szamosi discusses the contribution of music to the discovery of time as a fourth dimension in his article "The Origin of Time: How Medieval Musicians Invented the Fourth Dimension." He refers to Galileo's experiments with falling bodies that resulted in a mathematical formula based on the observation that "no matter how far the ball traveled, the distance covered was proportional to the square of the time passed. . . . Time came to be seen as a sovereign and autonomous dimension that stood apart from—and therefore could be used to measure—motion."[2]

Szamosi finds the source of this new concept of time in the polyphony of the twelfth century and the musical theories established in Paris. "It was at Notre Dame that the first polyphonic works for three and four simultaneous voices were written. . . . Centuries later, the baroque masters of the organ . . . would improvise polyphonic pieces during concert performances. And today, jazz musicians improvise several simultaneous melodies and rhythms without so much as skipping a beat."[3] Certainly, the musical concept of metered time that can control a diversity of melodies and rhythms has been a unique achievement of Western music.

This tradition was challenged in the 1950s not only by the recording of electronically generated sound on magnetic tape, but also by the introduction of serial techniques, which seemed at first to undermine the tonal functions of the temporal design. The Second World War had stimulated interest in other cultures and other aesthetic beliefs that also seemed to threaten the traditions of Western music. The 1950s demanded that the composer re-examine every aspect of his musical individuality.

This re-examination led inevitably to experimental fads. Indeed, experiment in music was considered the greatest virtue, and as a result, trends followed one another in rapid succession, adding enormously to all aspects of music except the traditional control of time and space. The most interesting experiments took place in popular music, partly, perhaps, because improvisation demanded metered time. The audience was able to follow more easily music that had a clear and even beat, just as football was popular partly because the time/space structure of the game was so clear.

The young composer of serious music at that time had a variety of choices. He could incorporate into his style devices that he found in American popular music, or he could return to old tonal devices, such as the organ point, dressing them up with slick electronic effects. The most experimental composers, and I think the most interesting, tried to find through electronic technology a new idiom that could express their musical ideas. A new vista opened up for the young composer, but for the older composer it was a period of agonizing choices.

The older artist faced a dilemma: he could turn back to his earlier musical concepts, or he could search for new concepts of time that suited his outlook. In doing the first he would become reactionary, but in doing the second, he might be accepting an aesthetic position that was untrue to his own personality. It took courage to grow old.

I found that the memory of earlier periods of my life brought to my music fresh ideas that shaped the form and affected both rhythm and melody. I became absorbed in the relationship of music to history.

Music can exist only in the present. Every time a work is performed, though it may have been composed many years earlier, it takes place in the present. Memory changes the past into the present. (Perhaps in science-fiction imagination changes the future into the present. I am unable to think of anything in music that is comparable to science-fiction.)

As a composer grows old, he seeks ways to find a new musical statement so that he will not repeat himself. If he fails to find a new way, his music will lack vitality and meaning and he probably will stop composing. With what awe one listens to the late works of Beethoven and Verdi and admires the courage of these masters as they faced old age. Both found a new statement that made their last works the climax of their lives.

Lewis Mumford argues that "man gains, through work, the insight into nature he needs to transmute work into artifacts and symbols that have a use beyond ensuring his immediate animal survival." It is through work that man is able "to continue the processes of growth and to postpone those that make for death."[4] During an individual's middle years, work is controlled by professional drives and obligations. "Man's capacity to impose work on himself . . . [gives] him greater security and freedom,"[5] but at retirement, after a lifetime of professional routine, it is hard to impose on oneself meaningful work. A new routine can result only from a changed relationship to time and space.

Few people are as professionally concerned as composers with time and space, but everybody is, to some degree, involved in making adjustment to them. For many older people, memories of the past are more vivid than present reality. To look back over one's life and consider the adjustments one has made to time and space may be good therapy for old age.

There is risk in looking back over a century. My musical obsession, so necessary a part of my life as a composer, seems less important in my eighties than it did two decades ago. Memory, also, has served its function. Is there something beyond memory that can give new importance to my remaining years?

Perhaps the experience of examining over a lifetime the changing functions of time brings about a synthesis that blends and relaxes the process. Memory may have brought about a change, but the capacity to look at one's own history may be the attitude that can give one the courage to grow old. Perhaps it was this synthesis that made the last music of Verdi and Beethoven so meaningful.

(1988)

19

Musical Complementarity

I sent my friend Frederic Goossen[1] a copy of an article that appeared in the Summer 1988 issue of *Daedalus*, "The Roots of Complementarity" by Gerald Holton.[2] I found it an illuminating survey of a subject that had interested me for a long time.

I've used the term "complementarity" when referring to my music without ever quite understanding what Niels Bohr was talking about. I got my ideas in the 1950s from talking to physicists like Robert Bacher of the California Institute of Technology and my journalist brother, Nathaniel S. Finney, who, in his reporting during the Second World War, met Bohr in Washington. I certainly knew nothing about the philosophical background of Bohr's theory.

Like many other composers in the fifties, I was forced to consider the split that had occurred with Schoenberg's introduction of a twelve-tone technique which had been placed dogmatically in opposition to traditional tonal theory. To the music critic of the fifties a composer was either a twelve-tone composer who wrote atonal music or he was not. A battle raged, and to a certain extent it still does.

There were several things that made this separation untenable.

I found no sense in the idea of atonality since I recognized musical form based on pitch polarity in many of the works by twelve-tone composers. This division thus seemed to me fabricated. I felt that it could be solved by using both ways of composing music, and I called that solution a system of complementarity.

The steps along the way to arriving at this solution are now somewhat vague in my memory. I suppose it all began with my first lesson with Alban Berg in 1932.

I showed him a new work I had composed, and he was very excited because the theme used eleven of the twelve notes of the chromatic scale. He quickly paged through the manuscript looking for the twelfth note, expecting to find it used at the climax. There was, of course, no such point since the idea had never occurred to me. Not finding the note, he lost interest in the piece. I realized from this experience that Berg was concerned in a work with functional points based on pitch.

He suggested that I analyze Schoenberg's Quintet, Opus 26, and showed me the row in the four forms on which it is based. He suggested that I use a different color for each of the four forms and that I do the transpositions on all twelve levels of the chromatic scale. In talking about these transpositions he often related the levels to the diatonic scale, such as leading tone, upper leading tone and mid-tone. I, II, III, IV, V, VI, VII, VIII became I, N, II, iii, III, IV, MT, V, and so on. I was confused by this as became apparent when I later made the chart.

Then he got out the Prelude to *Tristan und Isolde* and pointed out that in the first eight measures Wagner had touched on all twelve notes of the chromatic scale, and that a twelve-tone row existed if one omitted the repetitions that resulted from the sequential structure of the phrase. With a rather sly look, he suggested that we recompose the phrase using a strict twelve-tone technique for both the melody and the harmony. When he played the result he admitted that the Wagner sounded a good deal better.

After my lesson I analyzed the Schoenberg Quintet and found that it was in sonata form, with the first theme on the tonic, a bridge starting at measure 29 that moves through related levels to the second theme that ends on the dominant. My chart was a méss. I transposed down rather than up and therefore got all the numbering wrong. After correcting that I related the levels to the diatonic scale, which made clearer the traditional form of the Quintet. Berg never asked to see my analysis, which was typical of him as a teacher. He gave out ideas in his lessons and left it to the student to do the work or not, as he wished.

Berg's association of the twelve-tone technique with traditional tonal technique may have been a deep conviction or an attitude of the moment. I think it was a conviction and is the reason why his music is easier to hear than Schoenberg's. Important for me is the memory that Berg was not dogmatic about the technique and made no effort to isolate it from tradition.

The next step took place fifteen years later after my war experience in the Office of Strategic Services had made me feel that my musical vocabulary was inadequate. The shift took place between my Fourth String Quartet (1947) and my Sixth (1950). The Fifth String Quartet (1949) is much more chromatic than the Fourth, but the chromaticism is not adequately integrated into the structure. My Sonata no. 2 in C (1950) for 'cello and piano is similarly flawed.

In composing my String Quartet no. 6 in E (1950), I started a slow movement for violin and piano in which the theme was, though not consciously, a twelve-tone row. Then, at the end of the first phrase, I began composing strictly in the twelve-tone technique. I decided the movement wasn't for violin and piano but for string quartet, and in rewriting it for the four instruments the twelve-tone polyphony made sense. I decided I would use a different row for each movement. The first movement is based on a row very unlike the slow movement, and everything was related to it. I wanted the scherzo to be funny, so I chose a row that used the white notes followed by the black notes, thumbing my nose at the row technique. I decided in the last movement to return to the row of the first, in order to give formal shape to the quartet. When I finished that, I realized that there needed to be an introduction and a conclusion using all three of the rows at the same time.

It seemed obvious to me that the *large* form of the work was tonal and on E, but that the details of pitch continuity came from the twelve-tone row. The fact that there were now and then triads made me realize that triadic sonority had nothing to do with the large form and was merely one possible sonority in the pitch continuity.

Tonality as a word was, and still is, bothersome. In the macrostructure, tonality is really pitch polarity, related to, but not dominated by, the acoustical ordering of sound. The microcontinuity is really not structure at all, but motion from point to point. Pitches in a musical phrase, like words in a sentence, have different meanings depending upon the musical functions they perform.

This dualism in function bothered me, because study with Nadia Boulanger and Roger Sessions had led me to the conviction that *every note* of a piece should be analyzable from the standpoint of the tonal intention. (Is this Schenker?) Was it possible that no single system was adequate for analyzing these two different functions?

It dawned on me that in the job of surveying, a single line was inadequate for the location of an exact point. One had to have two lines that intersected to locate a point. The chromatic integration of the twelve-tone system might be made compatible with my strong commitment to tonality, if these two methods of analysis could be joined.

It was here that I began talking to my brother Nat and to my friend Bob Bacher and that for the first time the concept of complementarity arose. The situation in physics was not unlike the dualism in music: what could measure waves could not measure particles. For one, the classic Newtonian theory was valid, while for the other, the quantum theory was necessary.

This reasoning led to my acceptance of multiple functions in any phrase, the functions of pitch polarity or tonality, and of motion and continuity. It led me to the subdivision of the twelve-tone row into two symmetrical hexachords, and to a new recognition of the importance of harmonic rhythm.

I abandoned the idea of a twelve-tone aggregate and used instead a six-tone aggregate. (After all, a triad is a three-tone aggregate.) I found that I could achieve a harmonic rhythm of interest by varying the speed with which I moved from the aggregate of one hexachord to that of another. Because the two symmetrical hexachords result in a twelve-tone row, the potential for an interesting harmonic rhythm was increased, though the result should not, I think, be called twelve-tone.

Finally, as I became more eager in composing to refer to songs I remembered from my youth, I discovered a hexachord that was compatible with most pentatonic melodies—a hexachord that is related both to the circle of fifths and to the diatonic scale; in other words, a symmetrical hexachord that resulted in a twelve-tone row that had its roots in the ancient tradition of Western music.

Example 1:

Landscapes Remembered (1971) is based on this hexachord.

So the idea of complementarity has led me not only to justify the combining of systems that seem to many to be in opposition, but it has also given me a better idea of the musical functions that control time and space and a greater chance to make a personal, musical statement that can be heard readily.

(1988)

Part IV

Coda

20

Landscapes Remembered
Memory and Musical Continuity

You may have had my experience of giving a lecture many times, and suddenly finding as you're giving the lecture that it changes focus and becomes something new. I never did have a good title for this lecture. Finally I just gave it the title "Landscapes Remembered," which is the title of the piece of my music that I refer to in the lecture.

I was invited to serve as the American composer for the Second International Contemporary Keyboard Music Festival, scheduled for June, 1983, in Hartford, Connecticut, and in conjunction with the Festival I agreed to give a lecture.[1] I sent them the title "Landscapes Remembered," and their reply was: "What on earth does *that* mean?" I said, "Well, it has something to do with what I'm going to talk about, and it's also the title of one of my works." Still, they asked for something more, and I finally added "Memory and Musical Continuity." So the lecture became "Landscapes Remembered: Memory and Musical Continuity."

"Memory and Musical Continuity" always has been the real subject of this lecture. I try to draw from my music lecture ideas that have been generated from the composition of the work. Certainly this piece, *Landscapes Remembered*, is concerned with memory, and memory has become very much a part of my musical thinking over the last fifteen years. I think this may have started with the *Divertissement* that I composed in 1965 in Paris, which projects my memory of a "night on the town" when I was a student there in the 1920s. I guess it's forgivable, when you get along in your seventies, to have memories, very poignant memories, of the past. Memory becomes more vivid to you, almost, than the present. That reality is the basis of this lecture.

I have realized in the course of my thinking over the past fifteen years that one of the movements I have been involved in as a composer is a revolt against literary form in music, against the stranglehold that literary forms, literary space-shapes, have had on music. It has seemed to me that there should be a better kind of continuity available to the composer than simply to perpetuate literary forms.

Now, that subject in itself would supply material for a lot of lectures, and I find it somewhat embarrassing to get off on it; but the curious thing about my subtitle "Memory and Musical Continuity" is that it made me consider how terribly important aspects of memory have become in our time.

If you come right down to it, possibly the greatest changes, the greatest inventions, of this century have been concerned with the storage of memory. They are important not only in themselves, but in how they have influenced the *way* we remember. Take this example: When I was a youngster, a student in the 1920s, I had just three recordings along with their scores. They were *The Firebird*, *Petrouchka*, and *The Planets*. That's the only recorded music that had any meaning for me as a young composer in the twenties. Aside from those, every musical experience depended upon memory. I'd hear a performance, and I'd study the score, and I would retain the sounds in my memory. Before recordings, one just lived on the memory of past performances. Then recording developed, and all of a sudden the situation that had been normal for composers was changed completely, because for the first time you had a library, and you could listen to a work repeatedly. I do find that a record is, to a degree, destructive for me, because it destroys the poignancy of my memory of a work, and imposes instead something that I find flatter and not so interesting as memory. That's an example of the way in which recording has affected experience, has changed experience. The more one thinks of this, the more interesting become the ideas that arise concerning memory.

As I indicated earlier, this lecture is concerned with musical continuity, and with literary form. Maybe I should illustrate what I mean, because I now find even sonata form essentially a literary rather than a musical form. For instance, a perfect example of literary form is:

Example 1:

That's a totally closed form, a literary form. It isn't a musical form. Continuity in music doesn't arise in that way, but one does tend to imitate, to continue, the closed forms we have inherited. I think when he does, the composer denies himself a kind of continuity, a freedom of thought, that could lead to interesting results.

Connected with musical memory is the phenomenon of tonality. This is a fascinating aspect of memory within musical structure which I treasure very much indeed. It is the capacity a composer has to establish something that will be remembered throughout a work, and will influence what happens in its total span.

My work, *Landscapes Remembered*, was written because I wanted to write it. Many works are written because they are commissioned, but this was not. I wrote it simply because I wanted to, and intended it as a nostalgic "other-side-of-the-coin" to a work for band I had written earlier, called *Summer in Valley City.* I grew up out there in a small town in North Dakota—it's smaller now than when I lived there—Valley City, North Dakota. *Summer in Valley City* is humorous and light, but I wanted to write a companion piece that was nostalgic and a bit different. I also wanted to achieve a musical continuity that came from memory, but was not encapsulated in closed structures. I decided to do this much in the same way one does fade-ins and fade-outs in cinema, where first you have a focus, then it blurs, and then you move to another focus.

The way that a composition grows in my head is mysterious. I understand it less now than I ever have. But in *Landscapes Remembered* things began to take shape, and tunes, songs that I sang as a child, began to take shape, and I began to choose, or began to think of, folksongs—American folksongs—not bound by literary forms. For instance, if you consider the traditional version of "O Bury Me Not," you see at once that it's literary in form.

Example 2:

But the one I grew up with is not literary in form, and I decided that I wanted to use this version:

Example 3:

That song, which I admit I love, has the loneliness as well as other qualities I wanted. It is true that it's repetitive—obviously, it does only one thing—but it doesn't seem to me a literary shape. It seems to me to offer all kinds of musical possibilities. Now, also, take my version of "Barb'ry Allen." I'm not sure I know any other version, so I can't compare, but it seemed to me that "Barb'ry Allen" again is a song that is "open" in form, and would be interesting to pursue.

Example 4:

How was I to start using this material? It is obvious that you can't fade in and fade out musically unless you have a frame of reference, unless you fade out from something and can come back to something, and this, I thought, should be pitch. I felt there had to be a controlling central pitch. The memory of that pitch would have to be established in such a way that as you moved through the piece you would come to an awareness that you were "back home," or that you were departing, or that something had been put in that "disturbed the water," that things weren't clear any more.

I have worked since about 1960, or even earlier, from a symmetrical-hexachord idea. I don't believe that it's right to speak of my music as twelve-tone music, because I'm not interested in twelve-tone. I'm certainly not interested in that discipline. To me, twelve-tone discipline is obnoxious. The idea that all twelve tones are equal is preposterous to any musician, if only because a low note is certainly not equal to a high note. There is an enormous difference in overtones. So that seems to me an absurdity. However, I find that I'm also not interested in triadic harmony. As my friend Roberto Gerhard once said to me: "It was a very good capital investment for three hundred years, but it ain't paying as good dividends any more." However, I *am* concerned with tonality, though I don't think tonality has anything to do with triadic structure.

Tonality is pitch polarity. Tonality enables your listener to associate music with a pitch, a pitch which is often, though not necessarily, in the bass. I have no doubt that I got a lot of this from my teacher Alban Berg. I don't think you can understand his music as conventional twelve-tone music. If you try to analyze Berg's music from that standpoint, you miss an important aspect of it, that of its tonality. My music certainly has to be understood as tonal. That's how I became interested in the theory of complementarity that physicists have employed to understand the universe. What can be explained by Newtonian mechanics leaves a whole area that for explanation must use quantum theory. You can't approach such problems from one viewpoint any more than you can survey from one viewpoint. You must have two points that complement each other.[3]

It seems to me that in music, too, you have the factor that controls the minutiae, the microcosmic, and the factor that controls the whole, the macrocosmic. I find a symmetrical hexachord a very useful thing, and I wanted in *Landscapes Remembered* to use a symmetrical hexachord that would be compatible with folk material.

It's curious, you know, how these things happen. It didn't come, in this work, from a theory. It came from a sound on the instrument.

Example 5:

That sound, that cluster, I found fascinating. That cluster is this row:

Example 6:

My theory is that as long as you stay within the notes of the hexachord, either the first six or the second six, it doesn't make any difference what order of pitches you use. This procedure makes possible harmonic rhythm. Now, this row is F G A B♭ C D, and its complement is B C# D# E F# G#. The thing that fascinates me about that row is that it's just the circle of fifths, expressed as the fragments of a scale. *That* wasn't invented by Schoenberg or any other twelve-tone serialist.

Example 7:

I found myself particularly interested in this row because it seemed that it had interested composers long before the twentieth century. But there was another reason.

Most American folk songs that I grew up singing are pentatonic, that is, based on a five-note scale. This hexachord made possible the quotation of folk tunes.

Example 8:

Oh, bur - y me not on the lone prair - ie____,

So here was what I call a "geography," a territory in which this piece could take its life. Don't forget what I said earlier, that the music has to focus on a note, and in this instance the note it focuses on is D, the top note of the cluster. That D determines the pitch polarity of the entire work. It's not an ostinato in that it is repeated all the time—that I would find pretty tedious—but it's remembered all the time, so when you come back to the D you recognize it as being the most important pitch of the row, and thus of *Landscapes Remembered.*

There is another subject that arises in one's mind, with respect to *Landscapes Remembered*, and that is: Why does a composer quote? What is quotation in music? There has been very little understanding of this. If quotation is something you've gotten out of a book somewhere and grafted onto your music, or if it's to show that you're erudite and know this or that passage from Beethoven, it isn't very convincing. It seems to me that quotation must be concerned with psychological continuity. It reveals your inner thought, your inner consciousness, and you include certain things because they have conscious meaning for you. You might not be able to say precisely what that meaning is, and indeed, if you could say it in words, I think you should be a writer. I think quotation, somehow, must possess the immediacy of revelation for the composer. It must occur because it says something that has to be said at that time, and which can't be said in any other way.

Another thing to be said about quotation is that, if you've set up conditions in your music so that quotation is psychologically apt, you've reached the point at which much that you write will be thought by someone to be quotation even though it isn't. I've given you the only quotations that exist in *Landscapes Remembered*, but there are many places I could point to in the work where you might think I was quoting, especially when I use the trombone. (I don't know why the trombone seems to be guilty of this.)

I rarely read criticisms, but I'm going to read you the criticism that appeared in the *Village Voice* when *Landscapes Remembered* was first performed in New York. I read this because I think it's a good criticism. I'm not embarrassed by it; in fact, I think it shows that in one sense the writer doesn't know what's going on in the music, and yet he *does* know. I find it interesting. It's by a person whom I admire, the critic Tom Johnson, and he writes:

> Suppose you are listening to a nice string chord, and a harp arpeggio comes in, a bit like some 19th-century ballet score.
>
> And suppose that then the music shifts to a little folk-song fragment in the winds, and from there to a mournful viola melody played with a pinched sound.
>
> Then suppose that the music shifts to sustained tones, with everybody slipping in and out of tune as in some anguished Penderecki piece.
>
> Then suppose that a muted trumpet takes over with a light-hearted folk song, and that this leads to a few church bells followed by the long ominous ring of a gong.
>
> And suppose that this all takes place in only a few minutes.
>
> That's more or less what happened in Ross Lee Finney's "Landscapes Remembered" from the time I started taking notes until the piece ended.
>
> If someone had told me that a piece of music some 15 minutes long could change its mood this drastically this often and still hang together, I wouldn't have believed him. But Finney's piece proves not only that it is possible, but that one can create extremely sensitive music with such a totally discontinuous process. Much of the success of this work has to do with Finney's ear, his craftsmanship, his artful transitions, and his uncanny sense of timing. But I think another more mystical factor is at work.
>
> Finney says the piece is "based on memories of my childhood in North Dakota in the early part of this century," and I have no doubt that this is literally true. Otherwise the music wouldn't seem as honest and personal as it does, and it wouldn't cohere either. But all those disparate styles and melodies are somehow linked up in Finney's mind, and so, following some strange metaphysical path, they become linked up for us too. The listener can almost get inside the composer's memories somehow. I liked being there.[4]

I think that review is a revealing comment on the matter of memory and musical continuity, because there is a continuity in *Landscapes Remembered* that is different.

Now, I'm going to close my remarks by adding something which is unrelated, in a way. Almost always I begin a new work from something that I fall in love with in a work that I've just completed. I either become very fond of my works, or I forget all about them, but often I have to "get acquainted" with a recently completed work. That's one of the wonderful things made possible by recording. I begin listening to the completed work, and I will hear things that I know I never will do again in a piece, but also things that I just fall in love with. That happened with this piece. You probably never could guess what spot. It's where "Nearer My God To Thee" comes in, where I set it with vibraphone and bells. It starts with a low B–flat, and the melody is given to the violas *ponticelli.* It's very near the end, just before the return of the quarter-tones, the fade-out.[5]

Of course, continuity doesn't have to be achieved as it is in *Landscapes Remembered.* It could be a closed continuity. (You know, I didn't reason this way, I didn't talk to myself, I didn't think in those ways at all. It just began happening as I worked.) To cut it short: I wrote my Second Violin Concerto starting at that point in *Landscapes Remembered*, and evolving from that point. I think the connection is interesting, because the Concerto is not an open, but a closed, form.

I'd like to close by saying that it seems to me we're on the threshold of a wonderful breakthrough in music, and how much I envy the young composers who are starting out. It seems to me that what faces them are wonderful possibilities of musical form. There are so many things happening in this century that have affected musical form. I hope that every young composer will find his own personal continuity of musical statement, his own self, and will worry a bit less about what everybody else is doing. I believe that the solution for a composer lies within himself and in his relationship to the time in which he's living.

(1982)

Notes

1. The Composer and the University

1. Matthew Arnold, "Literature and Science," *Discourses in America* (New York, Macmillan Company, 1924), pp. 87-88. Arnold here quotes Friedrich August Wolf (1759-1824), German classical philologist.
2. George F. F. Lombard, "Self-Awareness and Scientific Method," *Science* 112 (No. 2907, September 15, 1950): 289-93.
3. Lombard, p. 290. Lombard here quotes James B. Conant, *On Understanding Science* (New Haven, Yale University Press, 1947), p. 37.
4. Lombard, p. 290.
5. Lombard, p. 291.
6. Lombard, pp. 291-92.
7. Arnold, p. 105.
8. Lombard, p. 292.
9. Merle A. Tuve, "Too Much Technology?," *Newsweek*, 30 (No. 21, November 24, 1947): 52, 54.
10. *Webster's New International Dictionary of the English Language*, 2d ed., Unabridged (Springfield, Mass., G. & C. Merriam Company, 1934), p. 1212.
11. Knud Jeppesen, *The Style of Palestrina and the Dissonance*, trans. Margaret W. Hamerik (Copenhagen, Levin and Munksgaard; London, H. Milford, Oxford University Press, 1927). Translation of *Palestrinastil,* Copenhagen, 1923.

12. Knud Jeppesen, *Counterpoint: The Polyphonic Vocal Style of the Six-teenth Century*, trans. with an introduction by Glen Haydon (New York, Prentice-Hall, 1939).

13. Allen I. McHose, *The Contrapuntal Harmonic Technique of the Eighteenth Century* (New York, Eastman School of Music series, F. S. Crofts, 1947). McHose's theory textbook, widely used and extremely influential at the time Finney wrote this essay, exemplified to perfection the faults the author found in so much textbook writing, although he refrained from identifying McHose or his book by name.

14. Percy Goetschius (1853-1943), well-known German-trained American music pedagogue. His numerous published volumes on such topics as *The Theory and Practice of Tone-relations* (1892), *The Homophonic Forms of Musical Composition* (1898), and *Exercises in Melody Writing* (1900) were models of pedantic strictness and rigidity.

15. Jacques Barzun, *Teacher in America* (Boston, Little, Brown, in association with the Atlantic Monthly Press, 1944, 1945), p. 319.

2. The Uniqueness of Musical Craft

1. Lewis Mumford, *The Conduct of Life* (New York, Harcourt, Brace, 1951), p. 56.

2. This remark is attributed to Mary Heaton Vorse (1874-1966), American labor journalist and novelist. Vorse was a friend of the novelist Sinclair Lewis. According to Lewis's biographer, Mark Schorer, in his *Sinclair Lewis: An American Life* (New York, McGraw-Hill, 1961), pp. 189-90, Lewis was fond of Vorse's observation, and delighted in quoting it all his life. Schorer gives this version: "The art of writing is the art of applying the seat of your pants to the seat of your chair." Schorer comments that Lewis used this variation of the quote in an interview: "A mighty important thing for all authors to cultivate is this thing Mencken refers to as 'Sitzfleisch.'"

3. E. M. Forster, *Aspects of the Novel* (New York, Harcourt, Brace and World, 1927), chap. 5.

4. Arnold Schoenberg, "Composition with Twelve Tones," *Style and Idea* (New York, Philosophical Library, 1950), sec. 5: 107. A revised edition, ed. Leonard Stein, trans. Leo Block, was published by St.

Martins Press, New York, in 1975. It is entitled *Style and Idea: Selected Writings of Arnold Schoenberg.*

5. Schoenberg, sec. 3: 105.
6. Arthur Burkhard, *Matthias Grünewald: Personality and Accomplishment* (Cambridge, Harvard University Press, 1936), p. 29. Reissued 1976 by Hacker Art Books, New York.
7. Burkhard, pp. 31-32.
8. Burkhard, p. 33.
9. Burkhard, pp. 38-39.
10. Paul Hindemith, *The Craft of Musical Composition, Book I: Theoretical Part*, trans. Arthur Mendel (New York, Associated Music Publishers; London, Schott and Co., Ltd., 1937). Translation, 1942. Rev. ed., 1945, p. 46.
11. Hindemith, *Craft*, p. 12.
12. Paul Hindemith, *Das Marienleben* (Mainz, B. Schott's Söhne and London, Schott and Co., Ltd., 1948), Preface, p. viii. The version of the English translation used by Finney in his essay has proved to be untraceable. A translation of the Preface by Arthur Mendel was issued by Associated Music Publishers, New York, in 1954. Mendel also supplied the translation in the program notes for the New York premiere of *Das Marienleben*, revised version, given by the New Friends of Music, Inc., on January 23, 1949, but Section 6, from which Finney quotes, was omitted from the program. Mendel's 1954 translation of the portions quoted by Finney is given below. It differs in detail from Finney's version, but resembles it closely.

On the basis of the old equating of certain keys with the expression of specific feelings: to symbolize certain regions of feeling in the listener with specific keys . . . I can even go further, and substitute for the equation *tonality = emotional state* a more far-reaching one, namely *tonality = group of concepts*, so as to widen enormously the field of tonal symbolism.

13. Igor Stravinsky, *Poetics of Music*, trans. Arthur Knodel and Ingolf Dahl (Cambridge, Harvard University Press, 1947), p. 63. A later edition, translated by Arthur Knodel and Ingolf Dahl, with preface by Darius Milhaud, was published by Vintage Books, New York, in 1956. It is entitled *Poetics of Music In the Form of Six Lessons.*
14. T. S. Eliot, "Little Gidding," in *Four Quartets*, 5, ll. 4-10 (New York, Harcourt, Brace & World, 1943).

3. The Value of the Abstract

1. John Locke, "Some Thoughts concerning Education," *The Works of John Locke, A New Edition, Corrected* (London, Thomas Tegg; W. Sharpe and Son; G. Offor; G. and J. Robinson; Glasgow, J. Evans and Co.; R. Griffin and Co.; Dublin, J. Cumming, 1823), 9: Sec. 197:191.
2. Locke, Sec. 203:195.
3. Paul Hindemith, *A Composer's World: Horizons and Limitations* (Cambridge, Harvard University Press, 1952), p. 3.
4. Hindemith, p. 4.
5. Hindemith, p. 4.
6. Shakespeare, *The Merchant of Venice*, Act V, Scene 1, ll. 64-65, in Lorenzo's speech to Jessica.
7. Ernst Cassirer, *An Essay on Man: An Introduction to a Philosophy of Human Culture* (New Haven, Yale University Press, 1944), p. 152.
8. Cassirer, p. 168.
9. Roger Sessions, *The Musical Experience of Composer, Performer, Listener* (New York, Atheneum, 1967, originally published by Princeton University Press, 1950), pp. 22-23.
10. Cassirer, p. 168.
11. William Blake, "The Tiger," from *Songs of Experience*, ll. 1 and 2.
12. Lewis Mumford, *The Conduct of Life* (New York, Harcourt, Brace, 1951), p. 27.
13. Susanne K. Langer, *Philosophy in a New Key* (New York, New American Library of World Literature, Inc., 1948, first published by Harvard University Press, 1942), Chap. 5, "Language."
14. Sessions, p. 5.
15. Aristotle, *Politics*, trans. H. Rackham (London, William Heinemann Ltd.; New York, G. P. Putnam's Sons, 1932; and Cambridge, Harvard University Press, 1967), Book VIII: 6:667.
16. Aristotle, pp. 663, 665.
17. *The Education of Henry Adams: An Autobiography* (Boston and New York, Houghton Mifflin, 1918), p. 80.

4. Education and the Creative Imagination in Music

1. Finney clearly is fond of this phrase. He quotes it, without attribution, in "The Uniqueness of Musical Craft." See note #2 for that essay.

2. Ernst Cassirer, *An Essay on Man: An Introduction to a Philosophy of Human Culture* (New Haven, Yale University Press, 1944), p. 168. Finney also quotes this passage in "The Value of the Abstract." See note #8 for that essay.
3. Cassirer, pp. 144-46.
4. Archibald MacLeish, "Dedication of the Carleton Library: Address Delivered at Carleton College, September 22, 1956," *Carleton College Bulletin* (No. 2, November, 1956), 53:12.

6. The Artist Must Rebel

1. Albert Camus, "Rebellion and Art," Part Four, *The Rebel: An Essay on Man in Revolt* (New York, Vintage Books, 1956), p. 253. First American edition (Alfred A. Knopf, 1954). A revised and complete translation by Anthony Bower of *L'Homme Révolté*, Librairie Gallimard, 1951.
2. Camus, p. 274.
3. Camus, p. 271.
4. Thomas Wolfe, *You Can't Go Home Again* (New York, Dell Publishing Co., 1960), pp. 519-22. Reprinted by arrangement with Harper Brothers.
5. Thomas Wolfe, "The Story of a Novel," *Short Stories* (New York, New American Library of World Literature, Inc., by arrangement with Charles Scribner's Sons, 1947), p. 120.

7. Making Music

1. Ross Lee Finney, *Making Music. Volume I: The Time Line* (New York, Henmar Press, C. F. Peters Corp., 1981).
2. Théodore Dubois (1837-1924), French composer, professor, and theoretician. Trained at the Paris Conservatoire, Dubois returned there in 1871 as professor of harmony. He became professor of composition in 1891 and director in 1896, retiring in 1905. His *Traité de Contrepoint et de Fugue* of 1901 exemplified the strictness and thoroughness of French academic musical education.

8. Modern Chamber Music in American Culture

1. Van Wyck Brooks, *The Flowering of New England, 1815-1865*, Rev. Ed. (New York, E. P. Dutton, 1936), p. 208. In Chapter X, entitled "Emerson In Concord," Brooks discusses the influence of Emerson, through address and essay, upon the imaginations especially of the educated youth of his day. His ideas here paraphrase those of Emerson in such essays as "Self-Reliance," "Compensation," and "Literary Ethics."

2. Review entitled "Whitman's Leaves of Grass," under "Editorial Notes—Literature," in *Putnam's Monthly Magazine of American Literature, Science, and Art,* 6 (September, 1855): 321.

3. This review, unsigned, appeared on the front page of the *Boston Post,* Saturday morning, May 19, 1860, vol. 56, no. 116.

4. Bliss Perry, *Walt Whitman,* in *American Men of Letters* series (Boston and New York, Houghton Mifflin, 1906), p. 121. This quotation comes from Henry David Thoreau's letter to Harrison Blake, December 7, 1856.

5. Perry, p. 99. Ralph Waldo Emerson, letter to Walt Whitman (Mr Walter Whitman), July 21, 1855. Whitman allowed Charles A. Dana to print the letter in the *New-York Daily Tribune,* somewhat to Emerson's annoyance, as he was not asked his permission. The letter has since been reprinted many times.

6. William Billings, *The New-England Psalm-Singer*, ed. Karl Kroeger, in *The Complete Works of William Billings* (Boston, American Musicological Society and Colonial Society of Massachusetts, 1981, distributed by the University Press of Virginia), "Introduction to the Rules of Musick," 1:32-33.

7. Billings, Preface to *The Singing-Master's Assistant*, quoted in David P. McKay and Richard Crawford, *William Billings of Boston, Eighteenth-Century Composer* (Princeton and London, Princeton University Press, 1975), p. 88.

8. Horatio Greenough, to Richard Henry Dana II, quoted in Brooks, p. 451.

9. Brooks, p. 452.

10. Brooks, p. 451. One can pursue Greenough's thought further in Henry T. Tuckerman, *A Memorial to Horatio Greenough* (New York and London, Benjamin Blom, 1853; reissued 1968), and in *Form and Function: Remarks on Art by Horatio Greenough*, ed. Harold A. Small with an introduction by Erle Loran (Berkeley and Los Angeles, University of California Press, 1947).

11. George Frederick Root (1820-1895), American composer and music publisher. Among his better-known works are the songs "The Battlecry of Freedom" and "Tramp, Tramp, Tramp."
12. Finney refers here to Sessions's Sonata no. 1 (1930), and String Quartet no. 1 (1936).

9. The Relation of the Performer to the American Composer

1. Andrew Adgate (birthdate uncertain, given variously as ca. 1750 and 1762-1793), church musician and choral conductor. A native of Philadelphia, Adgate founded the Uranian Society, later Uranian Academy, the purpose of which was to incorporate the study of music and singing into general education. His choral concerts included, among others, the works of William Billings.
2. Alexander Juhan (1765-1845), an American violinist and composer. Born in Halifax, Juhan pursued his professional career in the United States. He was associated with Andrew Adgate in the concert life of Philadelphia in the 1780s. For a discussion of the careers of Adgate and Juhan, and their sometimes acrimonious relationship, see O. G. Sonneck, *Early Concert-Life in America (1731-1800)* (Leipzig, Breitkopf and Härtel, 1907). Sonneck's book was reprinted by Musurgia Publishers (New York, 1949), and again by M. Sändig (Wiesbaden, 1969).

10. The Composer and Society: The Composer's Unique Relation to His Culture

1. The author's paraphrase of a statement from Theodore M. Finney, *Hearing Music: The Art of Active Listening* (New York, Harcourt, Brace, 1941), chap. 15, "How Music Talks," p. 171.
2. Roger Sessions, "The Composer and His Message," *The Intent of the Artist*, ed. with an introduction by Augusto Centeno (Princeton, Princeton University Press, 1941), pp. 122-23.
3. Horatio Greenough, "Structure and Organization," *Form and Function: Remarks on Art by Horatio Greenough*, ed. Harold A. Small, with an introduction by Erle Loran (Berkeley and Los Angeles, University of California Press, 1947), p. 121.
4. René Descartes, *Renatus Des-Cartes Excellent Compendium of Mu-*

sick: with Necessary and Judicious Animadversions Thereupon. By a Person of Honour (London, Printed by Thomas Harper, for Humphrey Moseley, 1653). The "Person of Honour" who provided the "Animadversions" upon Descartes was William Brouncker, Viscount (1620 or 21-1684), as editor.

11. Music and the Human Need

1. See "The Composer and the University," note #9.
2. Igor Stravinsky, *Chronicle of My Life* (London, Victor Gollancz, Ltd., 1936) (anonymous translation from the French), pp. 264-65.
3. T. S. Eliot, "The Dry Salvages," in *Four Quartets* (New York, Harcourt, Brace and World, 1943), Sec. 5, ll. 27-29.
4. Stravinsky, p. 92.
5. Stravinsky, p. 192.
6. Lewis Mumford, *The Conduct of Life* (New York, Harcourt, Brace, 1951), p. 53.
7. Mumford, p. 53.

12. America Goes West

1. Anthony Philip (Anton Philipp) Heinrich, 1781 (Bohemia)—1861 (New York). Composer of a wide range of vocal and instrumental works, including many with unusual titles inspired by his life and travels in America. Heinrich's career as a largely self-taught composer flourished chiefly in the United States, although he received some recognition in Europe. For more extensive treatment, and a list of works, see David Barron's article in *The New Grove Dictionary of Music and Musicians*, ed. Stanley Sadie, 20 vols., 1980. Reprinted with minor corrections 1981, 1984, 1985, 1986. (London, Macmillan Publishers, Ltd.; Washington, D.C., Grove's Dictionaries of Music; Hong Kong, Macmillan Publishers (China), Ltd., 1980), 8:441-44.
2. Finney refers to Adgate at somewhat greater length in "The Relation of the Performer to the American Composer." See note #1 there.

14. Analysis and the Creative Process

1. Hermann Scherchen, *Time* 73 (No. 1, January 5, 1959), 52.
2. Igor Stravinsky, *Poetics of Music*, trans. Arthur Knodel and Ingolf Dahl (Cambridge, Harvard University Press, 1947), pp. 63-65. Finney here interprets Stravinsky's position as expressed in these pages. See also note #13 to "The Uniqueness of Musical Craft."
3. Carl Jung, "God, the Devil, and the Human Soul," *Atlantic Monthly*, 200 (No. 5, November, 1957): 63.
4. Jung, p. 63.
5. Finney composed another work, *Edge of Shadow*, to a text by Archibald MacLeish, in 1960 on a commission from Grinnell College. In it, he used Row II which had been little used either in the String Quintet or Symphony no. 2. *Edge of Shadow* is scored for mixed chorus, two pianos, and a group of percussion instruments. The examples below outline the connections between the original row and the three works derived from it, as well as noting its origin in the half-step/whole-step trichord of the row employed in the *Fantasy* of 1958. All of these works are published by C. F. Peters Corp., New York. For a catalogue of Finney's works, see Edith Borroff, *Three American Composers* (Lanham, Md., University Press of America, 1986), Appendix B, pp. 280-86.

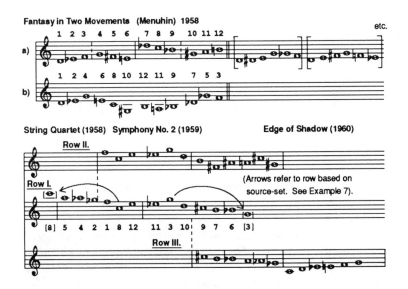

15. Problems and Issues Facing American Music Today

1. *The Orchestral Composer's Point of View: Essays on Twentieth-Century Music by Those Who Wrote It*, ed. Robert Stephan Hines, with an Introduction by William Schuman (Norman, University of Oklahoma Press, 1970), chap. 3, "Ross Lee Finney."

16. The Diversity of Inculturation

1. Roy Harris (1898-1979) discusses the matter of rhythm in American music at considerable length in his article "Problems of American Composers," chap. 21 in *American Composers on American Music*, ed. Henry Cowell (Palo Alto, Stanford University Press, 1933). Although he doesn't use here the simile of the taut rope that Finney

refers to, he discusses in detail his ideas of the differences between American and European concepts of musical rhythm, in particular the American fondness for asymmetrical rhythms and for syncopation based on internal beat-divisions. Harris contrasts these features of American music with the more metrical, conventional rhythms characteristic, in his view, of European music, including that of such major contemporaries as Stravinsky.

17. Composing Music for Dance

1. Finney's Chamber Concerto, subtitled *Heyoka*, is scored for violin, flute alternating piccolo, clarinet alternating bass clarinet, trumpet, bass trombone, percussion, and string bass. It was completed in 1981.
2. Geza Szamosi, "The Origin of Time: How Medieval Musicians Invented the Fourth Dimension," *The Sciences* (New York, New York Academy of Sciences, Sept./Oct., 1986), pp. 37 and 39. Article based on material from his book *The Twin Dimensions: The Invention of Time and Space* (New York, McGraw-Hill, 1986).

18. A Composer's Perception of Time

1. Lewis Mumford, *The Condition of Man* (New York, Harcourt, Brace, 1944), pp. 4-5.
2. Geza Szamosi, *The Sciences* (New York, New York Academy of Sciences, Sept./Oct., 1986), pp. 33-34. Article based on material from his book *The Twin Dimensions: The Invention of Time and Space* (New York, McGraw-Hill, 1986).
3. Szamosi, p. 37. Finney employs this quotation at much greater length in "Composing Music for Dance." See note #2 there.
4. Mumford, p. 5.
5. Mumford, p. 4.

19. Musical Complementarity

1. This essay appeared as a postscript to a letter to the editor of this volume. Finney headed it: "P. S. (one of the longest in history!)."
2. Gerald Holton, "The Roots of Complementarity," *Daedalus: Journal*

of the American Academy of Arts and Sciences, 117 (No. 3, Summer, 1988): 151-97. In this article, first published in the Fall 1970 issue of *Daedalus*, Holton explores the history of Niels Bohr's development of the seminal idea of complementarity in physics. Holton shows that scientific, psychological, philosophical, and theological influences combined in Bohr's thinking as he developed the concept. He is especially concerned to demonstrate that Bohr believed the concept had applications far wider than physics or the natural sciences. This fits in nicely with Finney's use of the term to refer to his original combination of large-scale tonality, or "pitch polarity," with small-scale pitch and interval continuity in his symmetrical-hexachord method of composition.

20. Landscapes Remembered: Memory and Musical Continuity

1. The Second International Contemporary Keyboard Music Festival was cancelled.
2. This and subsequent folksongs sung by Finney to illustrate this lecture demonstrate the flexibility of folksong as learned and remembered at various times in different places. For example, the text of "Pferdchen auf galopp" appears as follows in contemporary German versions: "Hopp, hopp, hopp, Pferdchen lauf galopp, Über Stock und über Steine, Aber brich dir nicht die Beine, Immer im Galopp, hopp, hopp, hopp, hopp, hopp." Finney says that he probably learned his version from his father who, though not of German extraction, knew and spoke German. There were, and are, many people of German extraction in North Dakota where Finney grew up.
3. Finney deals with the question of the relationship between microcosmic and macrocosmic musical structure at greater length in "Musical Complementarity." There, as in "Landscapes Remembered," he makes use of the surveying analogy.
4. Tom Johnson, "Music: Discontinuity hanging together," in the *Village Voice* (New York, November 7, 1974). From his review of a concert by the Chamber Music Society of the American Symphony Orchestra which included, in addition to Finney's work, Virgil Thomson's *Sonata da Chiesa,* and Edgard Varèse's *Integrales.* It was given in Carnegie Recital Hall on November 3.
5. Ross Lee Finney, *Landscapes Remembered* (New York, Henmar Press, C. F. Peters Corp., 1978), pp. 18-19, measures 232-38.

Appendix A

The materials collected in this book originally appeared as shown below:

1. The Composer and the University. Originally entitled "The Composer and the College." Lecture delivered in a course entitled The Contemporary Arts and Society, July 3-20, 1950, under the auspices of Summer Session Special Programs, University of Michigan, Ann Arbor.

2. The Uniqueness of Musical Craft. Unpublished address delivered as a Special Humanities Lecture, the first in a series of six, at the California Institute of Technology, Division of Humanities, Pasadena, January 18, 1951.

3. The Value of the Abstract. *The Voice of the Carleton Alumni*, vol. 22, no. 4, January, 1957, pp. 5-17. Publication of Carleton College, Northfield, Minnesota.

4. Education and the Creative Imagination in Music. *Education and the Imagination in Science and Art*, edited by Irving Kaufman, Department of Art, University of Michigan, Ann Arbor, and the National Commission on Art Education, 1958, pp. 42-49.

5. Employ the Composer. *American Music Teacher*, Journal of the Music Teachers National Association, Inc., vol. 11, no. 2, November/December, 1961, pp. 8-9 and 28-29.

6. The Artist Must Rebel. *Pan Pipes of Sigma Alpha Iota*, vol. 61, no. 2,

January, 1969, pp. 3-6.

7. Making Music. Unpublished lecture given at the Spring meeting of the Alabama Teachers of Music Theory, Jacksonville (Ala.) State University, April 16, 1983.

8. Modern Chamber Music in American Culture. *Volume of Proceedings of the Music Teachers National Association*, Thirty-sixth series, annual meeting of the sixty-fifth year, Minneapolis, December 26-31, 1941, pp. 79-86. Edited by Theodore M. Finney. Pittsburgh, published by the Association, 1942.

9. The Relation of the Performer to the American Composer. *Volume of Proceedings of the Music Teachers National Association*, Thirty-eighth series, sixty-eighth year, 1944, pp. 406-10. Location and dates not indicated. Edited by Theodore M. Finney. Pittsburgh, published by the Association, 1944.

10. The Composer and Society: The Composer's Unique Relation to His Culture. Address delivered March 14, 1948, at the Festival of Contemporary Arts, College of Fine and Applied Arts, University of Illinois, Urbana, March 10, 12, 13, 14, 1948. Symposium entitled "The Composer and Society."

11. Music and the Human Need. The *Pacific Spectator*, vol. V, no. 3, Summer, 1951, unpaged.

12. America Goes West. The *World of Music*, quarterly journal of the International Music Council of UNESCO, vol. IX, no. 2, 1967, pp. 22-30.

13. The Composer Speaks: The *Piano Quintet*. The *Michigan Daily*, University of Michigan, Ann Arbor, July 21, 1953. Originally entitled "The Composer Speaks: The New Finney *Piano Quintet*."

14. Analysis and the Creative Process. *Scripps College Bulletin*, vol. 33, no. 2, February, 1959, pp. 1-17. Publication of Scripps College, Claremont, Calif. Finney's address was delivered early in February, 1959. It has not been possible to establish the exact date.

15. Problems and Issues Facing American Music Today. *Student Musicologists at Minnesota*, University of Minnesota, Minneapolis, vol. V, 1971-72, pp. 121-31. Originally an address delivered at the Composer's Symposium, Music Arts Center, Indiana University, Bloomington, April 15, 1972.

16. The Diversity of Inculturation. Unpublished essay, 1987.

17. Composing Music for Dance. Unpublished essay, 1987.

18. A Composer's Perception of Time. Unpublished memoir, 1988.

19. Musical Complementarity. Unpublished essay in the form of a postscript to a letter addressed to the editor of this book, August 17, 1988.

20. Landscapes Remembered: Memory and Musical Continuity. Unpublished lecture given at the Region IV convention of the American Society of University Composers, The University of Alabama, Tuscaloosa, November 20, 1982.

Appendix B